Bill Hull

JESUS CHRIST DISCIPLE-MAKER

Church Ministries Department/Free Church Publications
Evangelical Free Church of America
1515 E. 66th Street
Minneapolis, MN 55423

TO
Jane, whose love, support, and objectivity
have kept me in ministry,
and
My sons, Bob and Kris,
who help me keep my perspective.

I would like to thank three people for their encouragement in my attempt to influence the Church for disciplemaking: Ron Broaddus, for his help in thinking through the original draft of **Jesus Christ Disciplemaker;** *Randy Knutson, for his role in implementing its principles; and Jim Westgate, for his encouragement and help in communicating the ideas on a broader scale.*

CONTENTS

AUTHOR

Bill Hull is currently pioneering a new Evangelical Free Church in the San Diego area. He has been a pastor in the Evangelical Free Church for nine years, serving congregations in Illinois and California.

He received a B.S. from Oral Roberts University and an M.Div. from Talbot Theological Seminary. Between college and seminary, he served on the staff of Campus Crusade for Christ.

Bill and his wife, Jane, have two sons, Bob and Kris.

FOREWORD

Bill Hull's book, *Jesus Christ, Disciplemaker,* is a breath of fresh air in our understanding of what it means to encourage others along the path of discipleship. Bill guides the reader on a walk with Christ through the short years of His ministry. With unusual insight, he draws significant principles from the familiar scenarios of the biblical documents. Discipleship is a logical socialization process involving time, exposure, sensitivity to readiness, and the modeling of truth. We become like the people with whom we associate. The pupil becomes like his teacher.

Quite frankly, I've grown somewhat weary of the term "discipleship." A grand biblical principle has been captured by cultural Christianity and distorted into a mechanistic, assembly-line process. I guess I'm tired of watching human rodeos—people herded into corrals, dehorned, vaccinated, branded, and put out to pasture. High-speed, short-term, results-oriented: we have turned the mechanics of ministry into the ministry itself.

But *Jesus Christ, Disciplemaker* turns our focus back to the very heart of our ministry to others. Although well written and easy to read, it is not a comfortable book. It challenges sacred assumptions and questions established methodologies. Most of the principles reach beyond theory to confront and convict. Jesus, our model, ministered with "both feet in the world," and He let the chips fall where they would.

Jesus Christ, Disciplemaker is a balanced, educationally sound attempt to redirect thinking back to a biblical model of discipleship.

Developing a lifestyle of leveraging people towards Christlikeness is what this book is all about. May God prosper its mission.

DR. JOSEPH C. ALDRICH
PRESIDENT, MULTNOMAH
SCHOOL OF THE BIBLE

INTRODUCTION

"Jesus came to them and said, 'All authority in heaven and on earth has been given to me. Therefore go and make disciples of all nations, baptizing them in the name of the Father and of the Son and of the Holy Spirit, and teaching them to obey everything I have commanded you. And surely I will be with you always, to the very end of the age'" (Matthew 28:18-20).

Before he departed from his disciples at the Ascension, Jesus gave them these practical directives for the Church. This was the Great Commission. Essentially, Jesus was asking his followers to spread the word of salvation to the whole world. But it is interesting that the action of the text here does not center on *going*. The participles *going, baptizing,* and *teaching* are all subordinate to the action of the main verb in this passage: the command to *disciple* or *make disciples*.

God's primary plan for the Church is for disciples of Jesus to develop other men and women into disciples!

There is probably no other more primary matter of negligence in the Church today than our failure to follow the Lord's command to develop disciples. Because of this gross neglect, many Christians think of themselves as an audience to be entertained rather than an army ready to march. The first century Church, composed of a tiny band of committed people, brought the mighty Roman world to its knees. In the twentieth century, however, it often seems that we who are many in the Church have allowed the worldly culture to disciple us into its way of thinking.

Only a minority of churches are focusing on what they should be doing, which seems incredible in light of such a direct strategy ordered by our spiritual Commander in Chief himself. The Church at large has ignored her marching orders. It is not that Christians are deliberately avoiding God's plan for the Church; rather, we have our focus in the wrong place.

Since indeed *discipleship* is the primary thrust of the commission we have been given, we must stop tacking it on our existing structure as a subordinate program in order to ease our guilt. Discipleship must function as the heart of church ministry. In fact, most programs should be evaluated in light of whether or not they are in some way contributing toward developing disciples.

The Greek word for disciple—*mathētēs*—means learner, pupil, someone who learns by following. The word implies an intellectual process that directly affects the lifestyle of a person. It is used in the New Testament primarily of "the twelve." Whatever making a disciple means, Jesus himself did it. Whatever a disciple is, the twelve were.

A disciple is distinct from an elder, even though elders should be disciples. A disciple is also different than a saint, although anyone who is a true disciple is a saint. A disciple is not just a church member, and yet church membership is indeed important for disciples.

Disciples span across categories such as age, interests, spiritual gifts, and theological persuasion. The factory worker, the college professor, and the housewife are all called to discipleship and disciplemaking; it is by no means the exclusive domain of the pastor. Christ wants to use the totality of his body in the discipling process. But why? What is it about disciples that is so crucial to the life and work of the Church?

The answer is nestled in a familiar illustration given by Jesus on the eve of his Crucifixion: "If you remain in me and my words remain in you, ask whatever you wish, and it will be given you. This is to my Father's glory, that you bear much fruit, showing yourselves to be my disciples" (John 15:7-8).

In this passage we see four characteristics that describe a disciple. First, he *remains.* Someone is a disciple only *if* he remains in Christ, consistently walking with him. Nowhere does the New Testament teach perfection in this lifetime. It does, however, teach *progress* in the Christian life. We grow as we immerse ourselves in God's message to us, for Scripture is the very heartbeat of God. Then, as we send up our message to him in prayer, the process of spiritual dialogue becomes more complete.

The second major characteristic of a disciple is *obedience.* On several occasions I have read the Great Commission passage (Matthew 28:18-20) aloud, intentionally leaving out two key words. Usually the omission goes unnoticed. The words "to obey" have been referred to as the great omission in the Great Commission. The great omission is that we have not really made disciples if we have not taught them to obey. There is no discipling without training, and there is no training without accountability. Indeed, God wants our love.

But love is primarily a verb, an action which is demonstrated through obedience (John 14:21).

The third basic characteristic of a disciple is that he bears *spiritual fruit.* If a person is remaining in Christ, established in God's word and prayer plus living an obedient lifestyle, he will inevitably bear fruit both in his attitude and in his actions. It is just as unthinkable for a disciple to be fruitless as it is for a healthy apple tree not to yield its natural harvest. You can indeed recognize a disciple by the results he produces in his own life *and* in the lives of others.

The fourth primary badge of a true disciple is that *he glorifies God.* Perhaps our foremost spiritual goal as disciples is to give God the glory he deserves. But we honor the Lord best by heeding his primary directive to the Church—disciplemaking. There is no other task or investment of our energy as crucial as this one.

But what is the best way to make disciples? Aha! That is the rub! We now launch out together to answer this pivotal question. And what better way to learn what it really means to be a disciple than to be instructed by the very first disciplemaker!

We will be going back in time, walking in the shoes of the early disciples. Our Instructor will not be teaching us of church programs, which are quickly modified in the tides of change. Nor will he sidetrack us with arguments about theological gnats. Rather, Jesus of Nazareth will teach us *principles* that transcend time and culture, principles of disciplemaking that can work in any setting, under any conditions. Yes, to be discipled—not by someone who may have forgotten the essence of those vital principles, but by the Master himself.

Part 1

COME AND SEE:
Evangelizing

Turning around, Jesus saw them following and
asked, "What do you want?"
    They said, "Rabbi" (which means Teacher),
"where are you staying?"
    "Come," he replied, "and you will see."
                                    John 1:38-39

1
THE HUNGER OF THE HEART

Beginning is difficult. Whether you're beginning a book, a diet, or a new job, it usually requires quite an effort to take that initial plunge. When Jesus of Nazareth embarked upon his ministry in the spring of 27 AD, he faced an awesome, complex challenge. Where and how does one begin the work of saving the world from total destruction, rescuing an entire planet that, for the most part, does not believe it needs help?

The Messiah-to-be made his first major move in an unlikely place, a dusty desert, and in an unlikely manner, submitting himself to baptism by an ascetic prophet named John. And yet the decision to go to John there in the desert was perfectly logical and appropriate, for John was the wilderness herald for the coming Deliverer—the Christ.

It was no mistake that John ministered in the wilderness,

for the wilderness historically represented the barrenness of Israel's spiritual life. The people of Israel had not heard from God in four hundred years. Thus they were progressively eager to have their Messianic expectations met throughout this period of severe silence.

The spiritual heart of Israel was parched, dry, and empty, much like the desolation of the wilderness. Thus when the Jewish people heard of this rugged young prophet trumpeting forth the words of the revered Isaiah, they trudged thirty miles out into the barren countryside to know more of his message.

John was the pioneer who preceded the Messiah, calling out to Israel, "Repent! Be prepared to encounter God!" Indeed, as Jesus walked toward him there in the wilderness, John pointed to him and openly declared, "Look, the Lamb of God!" indicating clearly that Jesus was the Messiah (John 1:29, 36). At this statement, two of John's disciples were immediately compelled to follow Jesus, without much thought for who or what they left behind.

Why did these men follow Jesus? Well, why indeed did *you* decide to follow Jesus? Hunger. Certainly curiosity is part of the motivation, but the hunger of the heart is the compelling force. This kind of hunger had been quickened in these men through the ministry of John. He had created in them a hunger for the Messiah—what he was and what he offered to Israel. As a result, these two men were drawn to the person of Jesus just as hungry animals are attracted to a source of food.

Throughout the past two millennia, many people have taken the same action as these two disciples of John, following Jesus to see who he is. Some of them were willing to follow all the way; others were not willing to pay the price. What is the price of discipleship to Jesus Christ? We will be following step by step along with these two men and the other ten to learn the answer to this question. The fundamentals of discipleship can best be grasped at the feet of the Master himself.

A prelude to commitment

The magnificent obsession of the Jew was to experience the Messiah, to witness the ushering in of the kingdom of God with all its promised benefits. John the Baptist spoke of the importance of preparing one's heart for the arrival of the promised Deliverer. The people came to him to be baptized as a sign of dedication as they waited for the coming King. An air of expectancy pervaded the land. Thus when John announced that Jesus was the Lamb of God who takes away the sin of the world, his disciples knew precisely what he meant. Their hearts were clean, curious, and cultivated by the Spirit of God.

John was serving in a ministry of preparation, provoking an interest in the Messiah to come. When Jesus, the true Messiah, arrived on the scene, John's season of preparation was over. He had successfully set the stage for the great event of salvation, but it was time for him to gracefully step aside.

Part of the discipling process is this phase of preparation, sustaining the believers while the seeds of commitment are germinating. We need to recognize the value of the work accomplished by someone like John the Baptist. He was an advance-man, a forerunner who prepared the way. Such a ministry is a natural prelude to commitment. In our churches today, we need to monitor and nurture the spiritual fledglings, as John did so well.

Typical ministries of preparation such as Sunday schools, music programs, and fellowship groups provide a forum in which the observant builder of disciples can watch and wait until a person is ripe and ready. Such programs are not to be discounted as non-disciplemaking ministries. But it must be recognized that they do not usually provide training in ministry skills.

These "holding tank" ministries are vital to successful discipling, for without them we would not have a primary opportunity to gather in those who are not presently prepared for more serious involvement.[1] We must be patient— waiting and watching for the proper moment. For the Spirit of God prepares the hearts of disciples for a certain moment when they stand up and say, "Here I am, Lord, reporting for duty." This was the case when the two men left John at the appointed moment to follow the Messiah.

An invitation to behold the Master

Jesus responded to these two men directly and somewhat abruptly. "Turning around, Jesus saw them following and asked, 'What do you want?' They said, 'Rabbi' (which means Teacher), 'where are you staying?'" (John 1:38).

Did Jesus really desire to know what they wanted, or did he already know? Certainly he was aware of their desires and expectations. They were filled with questions, and they needed answers. They possessed no plan; they simply stood before him on the threshold of hope.

Standing there staring at each other, they asked in bewildered unison, "Where are you staying?" In their awkward way, they were asking if they could tag along with him. Jesus answered with a simple invitation: *"Come and see."* In effect he was saying, "Come with me, and you can see how I live."

This invitation doesn't initially seem very significant. But with these words Jesus launched the first phase of his ministry. John 1:39 indicates that they stayed the remainder of the day with Jesus. We can only guess the content of their discussions, but we can observe that, as on many other occasions, they came away with their hearts aflame.

A vital principle of discipleship emerges at this point: do not recruit people for anything without first allowing them to have their curiosity assuaged. Jesus was not afraid to reveal the small print in the contract. We get the distinct impression from this passage that Jesus desired to make it easy to say no. He did not employ the misguided habit of twentieth-century Christendom of "quick-pitching" people into commitments. When this hasty method is utilized, the recruit normally takes off like a rocket, only to fall back later to the earth like a rock. After such a misfire, restoration is nearly impossible, a very messy business. We must not be intimidating when we invite others to take a look at the Master. Indeed, at the outset Jesus himself launched his plan to rescue planet earth with the simple invitation to come and see.

When people have their questions answered and fears reduced to an acceptable level, then they are ready to make a more committed move. This principle is illustrated by the shy and retiring disciple Andrew, who is always referred to as "Simon Peter's brother." Poor Andrew, always being overshadowed by big brother. When asked which musical instrument is most difficult to play, Leonard Bernstein answered, "Second fiddle." It is indeed a tough instrument to play, but one that is music to God's ears when it is played with dedication and humility.

Because Andrew was convinced that Jesus was the Messiah, he was willing to risk approaching his hardheaded brother about his discovery. Peter agreed to go with Andrew. As Peter stood there before Christ for the very first time, the Master demonstrated another key principle of discipleship. He said to the uncultivated fisherman, "You will be called Cephas," which means "Rock" (John 1:42).

As Jesus looked into the eyes of Peter, he saw more than meets the mere human eye. He knew that this was an impulsive, presumptuous, take-charge type, who would promise the moon and try anything at least once. Yet Jesus also saw a strong heart and a rare brand of courage. A man such as Peter, when filled with God's Spirit, becomes a rock of stability. Jesus saw a man who would stand strong several years later on the day of Pentecost, preaching the word boldly.

Jesus saw in Peter what he sees in each of us—nothing that a miracle cannot cure. Jesus sees his followers for what they will be, not for what they are in "the spiritual raw." Everyone is a candidate for something, and there are no exceptions. Regardless of what we might see in a person, pro or con, there is much more than meets the eye, things that only God understands. Here is a primary lesson for those seeking to recruit and develop disciples: *Do not depend on your own conventional wisdom. Seek the guidance of the Holy Spirit for spiritual understanding.*

With his heart aflame and his head filled with a motivating message, Andrew sought out Peter, and a chain reaction began. The next day Jesus found Philip, and then Philip found Nathanael. "Philip found Nathanael and told him, 'We have found the one Moses wrote about in the Law, and about whom the prophets also wrote—Jesus of Nazareth, the son of Joseph.'" Nathanael was somewhat skeptical, yet he agreed to at least take a look. It is interesting that Philip gave the same invitation used by Jesus himself, telling Nathanael, "Come and see" (John 1:46). This indicates the importance of modeling in just a small, embryonic way.

A basket, not a trap

Jesus had an ability to see into people's basic personality patterns. He often used this keen power of observation when he related to his disciples. To Peter, who wore an overbearing strongman facade (as evidenced in many impulsive attempts to impress the Master), he gave a boost in confidence.

For the skeptical Nathanael, Jesus demonstrated convincing proof of his extraordinary nature. Through his power of omniscience, he told Nathanael something that only one with supernatural gifts could know. His method was so effective that Nathanael soon became convinced of Christ's deity.

Jesus is adaptable. He speaks to people wherever they are and seems to understand, via sensitivity and divine insight, how to communicate with them.[2]

Jesus made one final point before departing for Cana, a promise indicating to Nathanael that he hadn't seen *anything* yet!

> Jesus said, "You believe because I told you I saw you under the fig tree. You shall see greater things than that." He then added, "I tell you the truth, you shall see heaven open, and the angels of God ascending and descending on the Son of Man." (John 1:50-51)

Jesus truly baffled them with this statement. Surely the disciples were not able to fully understand what kind of supernatural phenomena were to follow.

Jesus determined that the strategy necessary to rescue this planet from the clutches of the enemy involves *people*. This fact might seem so obvious that it need not be mentioned. Yet in the latter part of this century, there is perhaps no more blatant error among Christians than the dismissal of this simple idea. E. M. Bounds describes this very malady.

> We are constantly on a stretch if not on a strain, to devise new methods, new plans, new organizations to advance the Church and secure enlargement and efficiency for the Gospel. This trend of the day has a tendency to lose sight of the man or sink the man in the plan or organization. God's plan is to make much of the man, far more of him than of any-

thing else. Men are God's method. The Church is looking
for better methods: God is looking for better men.[3]

Most Christians believe that men are indeed the
method of Jesus, but precious few are willing to invest their
lives by putting all their eggs in that one basket. Believing
this people-oriented philosophy and practicing it are entirely
different matters. A large problem in Christendom is that we
don't want to take the risk or the time to invest in the lives of
people, even though this was a fundamental part of Jesus'
ministry. We fear that the basket is really a trap to ensnare us.

Every Christian needs to take time to select a few people,
and to determine to spend time teaching them the basic
fundamentals, such as Bible study, prayer, outreach, and
various ministry skills. But we must be careful not only to
teach the content but also to model these truths in our lives.
The *example* in outreach is vital; it serves as a catalyst. Each of
us should covenant together with one, two, or three others to
engage in weekly sessions for a fixed period of time.

But as we seek to reach others, we must keep in mind
that Jesus did not use manipulation or intimidation as a
recruiting method. He allowed God's Spirit to prepare the
heart. Indeed, the Spirit utilized John's ministry to prepare
certain men for the Messiah. Jesus himself never used high-
pressure or arm-twisting techniques. He truly made it easy
for people to say no.

A major problem of some Christian leaders today is the
"Let's whip them into a frenzy" syndrome. I use the word
syndrome by design, for when this style of motivation is
employed, it has to be used over and over again. It is tempting
in a church to utilize a motivational message, along with
effective music, followed by an emotional appeal for total
commitment. Yet when the music stops and the lights are
turned back up, the cold sweat of reality sets in. Such a

contrived, theatrical syndrome breeds superficial decisions and demands increasingly stronger tugs on the heartstrings.

I recently heard a missionary state that it is becoming more and more difficult to persuade the Christians of Western civilization to employ their Western wealth to assist the needy Third World. He went on to say that unless his video presentation of starving children has a few more oozing sores or swollen stomachs than the last film, the people in our churches do not respond.

Part of the problem is that we have manipulated and touched people only on the emotional level, thus limiting the long-term commitments needed to effectively change minds. If only we would take a simple lesson from Jesus—we might not gather such impressive statistics, but in the long run we would garner more solid choices by people moved by the Spirit.

Jesus launched his ministry with a simple invitation: "Come and see." During this inaugural four-month period, he allowed people to observe who he was and to learn what he planned to do. He answered their questions at length. But, even though he was indeed the Messiah, he did not force himself on the people of Israel.

Footnotes:
1. James Engel, *What's Gone Wrong With the Harvest?* (Grand Rapids: Zondervan), page 45.
2. Merrill Tenney, *John: The Gospel of Belief* (Grand Rapids: Eerdmans, 1948). Tenney points out that Jesus employed a multiplicity of methods in the twenty-seven personal interviews he engaged in, as recorded by John. Such a study is especially relevant in light of our present tendency to produce one-dimensional evangelists, disciples, and disciplemakers.
3. E. M. Bounds, *Power Through Prayer* (Grand Rapids: Zondervan), page 11.

2
EYES THAT BEGIN TO SEE

For people to catch a vision, they must first open their eyes. Spiritual realities are not easy to perceive, especially when one has spent an entire lifetime wearing spiritual blinders. Jesus said, "I have come into this world . . . so that the blind will see" (John 9:39). The context of this statement indicates that he was indeed referring to spiritual blindness.

It was Jesus' clear intention to fully but gradually expose his disciples to the nature of his kingdom. As we focus in on the second chapter of John, we observe the Master in the process of giving his disciples unique insights into some of the areas of life in which they had long been visionless.

The miraculous among the mundane
Jesus departed for Cana of Galilee with many new and curious men in his entourage. With the touch of an expert

discipler, Jesus ushered his trainees into a world they had always lived in but never fully seen.

The first major step on their journey lifted the minds of these men into a provocative new dimension. For there, within the festive but routine setting of a wedding ceremony, a miracle took place (John 2:1-11). Why did Jesus want to expose these men so soon to the supernatural? Because people need to be convinced of the presence and power of God if they are to catch the vision of his kingdom on this earth.

Jesus wanted to impress upon these men a full orb of spiritual realities so that they could make an intelligent decision about following him. The trip from the wilderness to Cana of Galilee provided at least a full day of discussion between Jesus and his starry-eyed novices. Never underestimate the value of a few hours in an automobile, for example, with a young Christian full of questions. As Robert Coleman said, "Never go anywhere alone; always take someone with you."

The disciples expected the people of Israel to unanimously recognize Jesus as the Messiah just as they had. Visions of ticker-tape parades in Jerusalem filled their heads. Thus they were not able to understand why Jesus chose a simple wedding as the next stop on the itinerary. But he had promised his mother that he would attend.

In John 2:3 we see that the unexpected happened: the wine ran out. Without hesitation, Mary approached Jesus concerning the problem. She had confidence that her son, being of sound supernatural power, would be able to handle this mundane, domestic situation. Jesus' response is curious: "Dear woman, why do you involve me?" In other words, "Why bother me with this?" Mary probably expected a miracle of some type, but we get the idea that Jesus was not too keen about such a prospect.

He then made a statement seemingly out of proportion to the situation when he said, "My time has not yet come," meaning, "I am not ready to reveal my full identity to the world at this time." This would become a common statement during the next three years. On several occasions Jesus was urged to follow certain courses that were in some ways attractive, and yet he realized that those choices would hinder his plan and purpose. However, on this occasion Jesus demonstrated both his flexibility and his devotion to his mother. Mary was persistent, and Jesus granted her request.

Flexibility in ministry is basic to success. Changes and compromises on minor points help to develop a common bond of mutual trust between colleagues. If people we work with perceive that we are not sensitive to needs when they arise around us, they will not want to follow us or dedicate themselves to a common task. If we are program-oriented rather than people-oriented, they will feel used and dispensable. They will see themselves not as viable ministers with value to the body of Christ but merely as another project.

Jesus proceeded to perform the miracle of turning water into wine, a miracle that designated his unique power (John 2:11). This was the first of many signs Jesus was to perform. The word "sign" in the book of John is pregnant with meaning. This Gospel is built around seven major signs.[1] After each of these signs, *faith* resulted.

Jesus gave these signs to establish a certain portion of knowledge and training in the disciples' minds. He did not perform miracles indiscriminately. Rather, he chose the situations carefully, interpreting and teaching his men the meaning of each.

Jesus walked by more sick people than he healed—not because he didn't care, but because he didn't want to leave the wrong impression about what is ultimately important. He wanted his disciples to understand that the deliverance of the heart and soul is far more vital than mere physical restoration.

The sign of water turning into wine revealed Jesus' glory, influencing his disciples to deepen their belief in him (John 2:11). This was their first exposure to the supernatural, but there was no mistaking what took place and who was responsible.

Christian leaders should have ministry antennae fully extended, utilizing ordinary situations in order to allow God to supernaturally intervene. For then people will yearn for more of the same, and they will grow in their commitment. Disciples should eventually come to a point of being prepared to deny themselves anything in order to be involved in the most exciting enterprise known to the human spirit.

Unfortunately, many of us move at a breakneck pace. We live in the "fast lane," passing by needs daily at very high speeds. As one caustic critic has said, "Jesus turned the water into wine, whereas the Church has turned wine into water." The glory of Christ has been seriously diluted in our experience, and thus the life we portray to the world is spiritually unattractive.

These disciples with their well-cultivated hearts now had seeds of the supernatural germinating in their souls, and, like so many others who have come after them, they would never be able to stop them from growing. This was the burgeoning of faith. Like blades of grass pushing their way through cracks in the sidewalk, the seeds of thought were maturing, steadily changing the lives of these men. As disciples who are commissioned to train others, we should perpetually expose people to the supernatural, extending both them and us. We need to reach out to accept the daily challenges that place us in positions of nurturing and motivating others.

Identifying the enemy

It often helps our understanding of what we should be like or what we should be doing if we are exposed first to what we should *not* be doing. When Jesus entered Jerusalem in 27 AD for the first of four consecutive Passovers, he clearly demonstrated this teaching (John 2:13-22). This was the first of two major confrontations taking place at the temple there. The second took place directly before his crucifixion three years later.

A repugnant practice had been adopted in the temple by some of the religious leaders of Israel. Jesus became angry when he walked into the temple courts and saw money changers selling sacrificial paraphernalia to travel-weary pilgrims. The priests reasoned that since donations were down and since Jerusalem would swell to nearly one million in population during Passover, it would be wise to go into business for themselves by opening up their own markets in the "Court of the Gentiles." After all, who cared about Gentiles anyway—they weren't important!

And so these "religious" men transformed the Court of the Gentiles into a bazaar, with stalls for the animals and tables for various other materials. One could only imagine how it looked, sounded, and smelled. What a perverse carnival, with these men in the temple exploiting the spiritual needs of the people for their own selfish gratification.

The Court of the Gentiles was supposed to be used for prayer and meditation, and moreover for evangelization of the Gentiles (Mark 11:17). What an ugly spectacle for the Son of God to see! The evangelistic outreach of the temple had been sacrificed at the altar of the almighty dollar! Greed had consumed many of the Jews. They had forgotten their very reason for being. They had become more concerned for themselves than for the lost.

Such corruption, of course, cannot be limited to the first

century. There is a propensity among fallen man to tamper with the design ordained by God for his people, a propensity that has been evidenced throughout the course of Church history.

The disciples had seen Jesus laugh, pray, express deep love, and perform great miracles. But they had not yet witnessed his white-hot anger. The whoring life of the woman at the well, the timid hypocrisy of Nicodemus, the adultery of the woman thrown at his feet—none of these sins provoked Jesus to vent his wrath. The primary catalyst of his rage was the leaven of the Pharisees. This leaven was their hypocrisy, their exploitation of human need for personal gain, and their abuse of what was sacred and holy. And so Jesus grabbed a whip and cried out to the animal merchants in a voice filled with holy tension, "Get these out of here! How dare you turn my Father's house into a market!" (John 2:16). And then he proceeded to rip the bazaar apart.

Many religious trappings and abuses have infiltrated the body of Christ today. To interpret this as a warning against selling tickets to the church missionary dinner in the lobby is to totally miss the point. Rather, it is more like a warning not to sell communion wafers in the sanctuary.

But what has happened to us in the twentieth century is far more subtle. Satan is too smart to rattle his sabers, engaging in a frontal attack. He would much rather use a less threatening yet more effective technique in the form of a *principle*. The deceiver works through principles because they bridge both culture and time. The same principle can be camouflaged so that it looks different from one time to the next.

The principle employed by the enemy there in the Court of the Gentiles was the transforming of the mechanics of ministry into the ministry itself. We often see this inclination in sincere churchmen who find ultimate meaning in filling out forms, voting on issues, and determining the proper application of Robert's Rules of Order. In such cases the church budget becomes the standard by which all decisions are made. Unfortunately, good people get totally wrapped up in these issues, forgetting the importance of Bible study, prayer, and outreach.

Once a young sculptor fell deeply in love with the woman of his dreams. They were made for each other, having similar interests, sharing values, and agreeing on the priorities of life. A wedding took place, and the marriage was as fresh and exciting as the courtship.

However, tragedy struck when it was found that she had an incurable disease. After his wife's death, the artist desired to dedicate a work of art to her memory. He created a magnificent sculpture that was chosen to adorn a new plaza in the middle of town. The work was instantly popular, so much so that the young artist's work was all at once in great demand.

A year later several more of the young man's works were added. He became so well known that art lovers would travel from throughout the region to view his work. Eventually the plaza area was so cluttered with art pieces that some of them had to be removed. A friend asked what the piece of work in the center of the plaza was intended for, since it was the least popular of all the sculptures. The young artist agreed that it looked out of place and ordered it removed. What was once the centerpiece of his work and his driving force had become unimportant and obsolete. Thus it was replaced.

This is what had happened to many of the spiritual leaders of Israel. The Court of the Gentiles, where once men of other nations could come to seek after God, had now been turned into a place of exploiting the need of serious worshipers. Although the mechanics of ministry are necessary attachments to the ministry itself (without them, most ministries would be ineffective), I have known faithful church members who were better acquainted with the church constitution than with Scripture. Misguided Christians often place an inordinate amount of importance on who is in control and who has the authority. They become preoccupied with their power rather than their responsibility. This is what happens when mechanics become as important as the actual ministry itself. In the process, the true spiritual essence is lost.

Jesus was angered because the spiritual leaders of Israel, who were supposed to be a light to a darkened and alienated world, were consumed with meeting their own needs. As a result, they sacrificed their outreach to the world.

Many churches across America, like the leadership of Israel, have forgotten the reason why the Church exists. Statistics on evangelism indicate that less than fifty percent of the evangelical churches in America have an organized outreach.[2] This is a sad fact of spiritual pathology for the Church, which was intended to be a living organism reaching out to a needy world.

If we gave Jesus an opportunity, he would once again take whip in hand and rampage through our religious dwellings, crying out, "Get these out of here—these cold, calculating spirits that are more concerned about being right than meeting needs, that make the mechanics of ministry the ministry itself! Take it all away! Clear the decks and start fresh!"

Many churches simply need to reorganize themselves so that the biblical priorities can be fulfilled. The key is to release the strongest leaders from the shuffling of papers and the maintenance of the machinery of the church to the freedom of ministering directly to *people*. Such a strategy inevitably strengthens the body of Christ.

Jesus recognized and confronted the enemy there in the temple. And what effect did this cleansing of the temple have on the disciples? "His disciples remembered that it is written: 'Zeal for your house will consume me'" (John 2:17). These men, raised in Jewish homes where the Scripture was revered, recalled the words of the psalmist from their childhood (Psalm 69:9). This act of recollection might seem unimportant at first, yet it represents part of the spiritual compass Jesus wanted to instill into these men during this introductory exposure—the "Come and see" phase. The word of God worked in their spirits to help them put the pieces of the Messianic puzzle together. Each piece that was added to the puzzle worked within them, deepening their conviction.

The religious leaders in the temple struck back defensively at this seemingly presumptuous, unlettered maverick.

Then the Jews demanded of him, "What miraculous sign can you show us to prove your authority to do all this?"

Jesus answered them, "Destroy this temple, and I will raise it again in three days."

The Jews replied, "It has taken forty-six years to build this temple, and you are going to raise it up in three days?" But the temple he had spoken of was his body. (John 2:18-21)

Perhaps this was the first opportunity for the disciples to observe Jesus doing battle with the lettered leaders of Israel. They were no doubt curious about how Jesus would fare against these giant intellects. It is always important for disciples to be assured that their spiritual leader can stand the scrutiny of opponents.

The Jews there in the temple questioned Jesus' authority with the kind of evasive logic typical of most carnal religious leaders: *What committee okayed this?* The answer from the

Master is both profound and priceless, but it was nonsense as far as the Pharisees were concerned: "Destroy this temple, and I will raise it again in three days." They thought he was talking about reconstructing Herod's temple. Not only did this fellow appear to be unlettered and violent, but he also seemed to be somewhat insane. But, as usual, what Jesus had in mind was much too profound for these narrow minds.

"The temple he had spoken of was his body" (John 2:21). Apparently nobody understood what he meant except Jesus himself. But the Messianic puzzle would eventually come together piece by piece. The Lord told his disciples, "The Holy Spirit . . . will teach you all things and will remind you of everything I have said to you" (John 14:26). Indeed, after Jesus was resurrected his disciples remembered what he had said about raising the temple in three days (2:22).

Jesus used every situation as an opportunity to teach his disciples. Class was always in session in the laboratory of life. This unique Teacher did not mind planting seeds of thoughts early, even if those seeds involved disjointed statements or in the end left bigger questions than were originally asked. Jesus did not subscribe to the "storage tank" approach to education that is the primary motif of the Western world. The storage tank philosophy is to stockpile large quantities of information in the minds of students in a short period of time. Jesus preferred planting a few seeds of thought and then nurturing them through experience.

Consider the story of a young boy who desired to become an authority on jade. He approached his local jade expert to inquire about an apprenticeship. The master instructed the boy to simply come to his house the next day and the lessons would begin.

The boy faithfully reported daily for his lessons. But he grew somewhat impatient and confused when all the master had him do was sit for several hours with a piece of jade in his hand. After some months and much frustration, the young boy determined to ask his teacher when he would actually begin to learn about jade. The master simply answered, "Come back tomorrow."

Upon his arrival the next morning, nothing seemed to be different. The boy reported to his usual spot, and the jade master took a stone and placed it in the hand of the young boy. As the stone touched the boy's hand, he jumped up, dropped the rock, and cried out, "This is not jade!" How did he know, for the jade master had not spoken a word concerning jade? Yet the boy understood what only an expert could know. He had, through experience, come to a knowledge that no textbook or lecture could have provided.

This does not discount textbooks or lectures. Jesus himself used a text (the Old Testament) and lectured on a regular basis (the Sermon on the Mount and the Upper Room discourse). But the cement of knowledge comes only through the application of truth brought alive by experience. Jesus must have understood quite well the ancient proverb, "I hear, I forget; I see, I remember; I do, I understand."

As the disciples walked away from the temple that day, they had learned empirically that there was an enemy to be contended with, and that his purpose was to pervert the truth of God's redemptive plan. We can see the enemy wherever we go, even in a place of worship.

Turning the gaze inward
The next few days in Jerusalem served as a kaleidoscope of wonder for the disciples. The holy city's expanded holiday population provided Jesus with the right kind of variety of human need to demonstrate both his desire and his ability to help people. Within this setting the disciples could see clearly the content of Jesus' heart.

To be an effective motivator and builder of others, one

must possess the right motivation within. The disciples were convinced that Jesus had the proper credentials—John the Baptist himself had endorsed him, he was of the proper pedigree (the tribe of Judah, the family of David, born in Bethlehem, etc.), and furthermore his authenticity seemed to be resoundingly verified by the many miracles he performed. And yet did he really care about people?

The disciples had several opportunities to see Jesus' inner character. They observed his humility as he submitted himself for baptism before John. They looked on as he showed respect for his mother at the wedding reception. They beheld his courage when he confronted the powerful religious leaders and intellectuals of his day. But the most impressive dimension of his identity was that he *loved*—he loved his Father and he loved people. Jesus was a warm man who was willing to spend hours ministering to the "have-nots," the down-and-outers, those to whom other religious leaders would not give the time of day. The disciples saw in this miracle-worker a caring and consistent love that defied description.

But what was his motivation? Was he trying to impress the people of Israel with all those miracles? Scripture gives the answer: "Jesus would not entrust himself to them, for he knew all men. He did not need man's testimony about man, for he knew what was in a man" (John 2:24-25).

We can learn greatly from the temptations Jesus encountered in his ministry. He experienced great popularity during the early stages of his ministry. Many who witnessed his miracles were captivated; they believed in him and wanted to follow him (verse 23). If he had allowed it, this excited multitude would have rounded up a white stallion, a golden chariot, a purple sash, and a laurel wreath for a crown, and then they would have hoisted Jesus onto the animal and paraded him through the streets of Jerusalem.

But Jesus resisted this temptation firmly throughout his life until the very end. As his popularity grew, even his closest disciples advised him to allow himself to be ushered in as the recognized leader of his people. Much later in Christ's ministry, during the Feast of Tabernacles, he resisted the pressure of his own brothers to go public by simply stating, "The right time for me has not yet come" (7:6).

The multitudes actually attempted to take Jesus by force as their king (John 6:15). Even the Pharisees admitted that just about everybody seemed to be following this apparently blasphemous maverick (12:19). But Jesus resolutely resisted all such attempts to change his agenda. He kept a low profile, thus demonstrating to his disciples the importance of humility. He "would not trust himself to them"—in other words, he was not going to allow his destiny and his mission to rest in the hands of others (2:24). The Man had to count the cost himself, considering the value of what he was buiding. He wasn't just living for himself or for his own generation; he had to think of the people of the many generations yet to come.

The Messiah would not allow the weakness of human flesh to control his destiny. Jesus, knowing that the commitment of the crowds was largely superficial, determined that he could not build the future on something so insubstantial. His reasoning was eventually verified. For later, when Jesus told the crowds of the true cost of discipleship (John 6:60-71), many people scattered after hearing the requirements.

The Messiah's standard operating procedure when confronted with pressure to go public and to allow the will of the people to prevail was simply to withdraw from the situation (John 6:15). His ability to electrify the multitudes created a serious problem for Jesus: It tended to cause a distraction from the main thrust of his ministry, thus endangering its cutting edge.

Satan wants to dull the cutting edge of Christian leaders by tempting them with popularity and fame. He seeks out the most effective leaders in the local church, skimming the cream off the top by sidetracking them in the limelight of some cosmetic, meaningless ministry. The result is that the most effective builders of men are displaced from the local setting and made into "Christian personalities."

Often the most effective doers of ministry are relegated to the tasks of giving messages or doing administrative work rather than the task of building disciples in the local setting. Certainly there is a place for all dimensions of ministry, yet we need to determine carefully our priorities according to God's priorities. Sometimes we need to turn our gaze inward to determine whether or not our primary motivation is right.

Jesus was not duped by the pull of popularity. He knew that the masses were like sheep, following anyone who met their immediate needs. Much of the modern world is like this flock of sheep.

> It is not difficult in such a world to get a person interested in the message of the gospel; it is terrifically difficult to sustain the interest. Millions of people in our culture make decisions for Christ, but there is a dreadful attrition rate. Many claim to have been born again, but the evidence for mature Christian discipleship is slim. In our kind of culture anything, even news about God, can be sold if it is packaged freshly: but when it loses its novelty, it goes on the garbage heap.[3]

There is a propensity in society toward fads in fashion, foods, and films. An even more dangerous aspect of fickleness is evidenced in the rise of cults and aberrant religious groups.

The pertinent question here is, How can we, like Jesus, resist the temptations to be placed on a pedestal? Jesus knew exactly what his mission entailed, therefore he would not allow himself to be deterred. In this sense he was a man of one idea, interested in building up a few select men who would in turn perpetuate the Church.

Jesus believed in spiritual multiplication. He took the long view of what was necessary for a strong movement. The patient training of disciples is the only means unanimously endorsed by Scripture for building the Church. In contrast, we see in the twentieth century the shortcut, pragmatic approach. When churches try one crash program after another without strengthening the body of disciples, volumes of time and energy are wasted. If our ministries do not lead to the making of obedient fruit-bearing believers, then we have simply "fattened up" the Church.

Those who have solid Christian character should be reaching out to others in evangelistic and nurturing ministries, thus helping them develop their character. But disciples must always beware the detours of pride. The push to be successful is so strong that most leaders find it excruciatingly difficult to follow through with the courage of their convictions. This ongoing spiritual battle brings new meaning to the words of Paul: "I die every day" (1 Corinthians 15:31). All who desire to follow Jesus must be stalwart disciples, standing strong against all diversions, dying to self-indulgence. True disciples learn and relearn many times from the example of Jesus that to do the will of the Father and to stay on *his* agenda is more productive than the most attractive of alternatives. This is a vital lesson in humility.

The eyes of Jesus' disciples were opened to a whole new approach to life. As the disciples observed the miracles performed by Jesus, they grew in faith. As they watched the spiritual enemy try to undermine the outreach of ministry, they grew in discernment. And as they came to see the importance of integrity of character for spiritual effectiveness, they grew in humility. Early in the course of discipleship, the seeds are naturally just starting to germinate. But the process of spiritual multiplication begins small and then expands exponentially with great acceleration as each part of the body of believers works to increase the harvest.

Footnotes:

1. Tenney, *John*, page 312. Tenney's list of seven major signs is as follows: (a) water into wine (2:1-11); (b) healing of the official's son (4:46-54); (c) healing at the pool (5:1-18); (d) feeding of the five thousand (6:1-14); (e) walking on water (6:16-21); (f) healing of the blind man (9:1-41); (g) raising of Lazarus (11:1-44).
2. *Christianity Today* article on Gallup poll.
3. Eugene Peterson, *Long Obedience in the Same Direction* (Downers Grove, Illinois: InterVarsity), page 12.

3
CREATIVE PERSUASION

As creatures made in the image of God, we are beings of creativity. Within our souls we desire to satisfy that part of our nature that constantly hungers for something new. When things are always done in the same old way, we inevitably get bored.

The spiritual frontier is constantly teeming with new challenges, obstacles, victories, and tragedies. There is nothing boring in the uncharted territory to which the followers of God are called. But as the message of deliverance is carried to the world, it seems that often people are unchallenged and bored by the very news that should indeed excite their souls. And yet at the same time we should recognize that if the ones who deliver the message are bored, the ones who hear it will probably be bored as well.

A disciple is a messenger of God. The way the disciple

presents the message determines to some extent the effectiveness of God's communication to man. Consequently, a
creative, honest approach to evangelism is vital to the success of the Great Commission.

Jesus was a creative communicator. He did not use the
same approach with every person. Because he realized that
all people are to some extent unique, Jesus was imaginative
and flexible in his evangelism techniques.

Evangelizing the religious establishment

Jesus was always ready to relate to a person's frame of
reference (the cultural, educational, and environmental factors that shape one's thinking) in a creative way. He used
four word pictures in John 3:1-21 that give evidence of his
creative evangelism: (1) spiritual birth is akin to physical
birth; (2) the Holy Spirit's activity is like the wind; (3) the
death of Christ is like the snake being lifted up in the
wilderness; and (4) the effect of the new birth is like light
shining in darkness.

Nicodemus was part of the conservative religious establishment—a Pharisee who held a position in the Sanhedrin. The Pharisees were opposed to Jesus because he posed
a threat to their treasured legalistic way of life and their
interpretations of the Messianic passages of Scripture.

Nicodemus came at night for he feared that others
would learn of his interest in Jesus. He was probably convinced by the signs Jesus was performing that there was
something special about this particular religious teacher.
John the Baptist had spoken about a repentance that prepares the heart for redemption. Then along came Jesus
saying that the kingdom of God is among the people and
that redemption is imminent. These messages had created a
thirst for new life in this old Sanhedrin sage.

Nicodemus was extremely polite and complimentary as

he began to speak with Jesus. But before he could ask a question concerning eternal life, Jesus gave the answer:

> "Unless a man is born again, he cannot see the kingdom of God." (John 3:3)

This is the first of four word pictures. Of course, this creative image caused Nicodemus to ask the obvious question: How can an old man be born all over again? It is clear that Jesus had piqued his curiosity via this vivid illustration of spiritual birth. It conveys the idea of a fresh start, something new and exciting.

Jesus mentioned three times the importance of being "born again" (verses 3,5,7). This illustration must have struck Nicodemus with a sense of irony, for the older a man is (according to the Pharisees), the wiser, the more learned, and closer to God he is. Jesus plunged his dagger of truth into the heart of this attitude, saying in effect, "Nicodemus, you need to start over again!"

Jesus moved right into his evangelistic presentation because he understood the Pharisaic frame of reference. He did not try to share with Nicodemus everything he knew about God, the Bible, and the universe in one sitting. Rather, he hit him right in the most relevant and vulnerable spot.

Although Jesus was capable of plunging right in, usually we are not. Because he was omniscient, he understood the thoughts and questions swimming about in people's heads. The average Christian, however, must take time to listen and learn the questions that a person is asking, and must then be willing to give honest answers to honest questions. Sensitivity to the leading of God's Spirit and to the thinking of each individual person is vitally important. Also, a disciple should always be prepared with at least one system of witnessing, so that when the opportunity presents itself, he will not be left with nothing intelligent to say. Every Christian has the responsibility to be able to share the gospel in a clear and concise fashion. It is the person who knows *the basics* who can readily adapt to the unusual and special circumstances.

The second word picture Jesus presented to Nicodemus followed naturally out of the first:

> "The wind blows wherever it pleases. You hear its sound, but you cannot tell where it comes from or where it is going. So it is with everyone born of the Spirit." (John 3:8)

In so many words Jesus told the perplexed old man, "I don't expect you to understand spiritual birth, Nicodemus. It's like attempting to bottle the wind: it blows where it wishes. You don't know where it came from nor where it is going. You can't see it, smell it, or get a handful of it. However, the results are easily discovered: the rustling of leaves, the turning of a windmill, the destruction after a wind storm." Spiritual birth is supernatural. Trying to "box up" the Spirit is not only spiritually dangerous but also impossible. It is interesting to note that the Greek word for *spirit* is the same word as *wind*.

The response of Nicodemus was simple: "How can this be?" (3:9). One weakness that I have observed in those of us dedicated to the process of "no nonsense" building of disciples is a tendency to try to surround the Holy Spirit, keeping him under control. I find in myself a subtle but sure desire— not to quench the Spirit, but to control the Spirit. Disciplers sometimes work with charts, graphs, plans, and strategies. The results, at times, can be that we are so immersed in the details of the discipling process that we lose some of the spontaneity that is available to those who are sensitive and flexible in relation to the Spirit's leading.

Let us not rip the mystery out of discipleship! We should

be careful not to become "Johnny one note" evangelists who develop tunnel vision as they work with others. A discipler must not have a fixed idea of what a disciple looks, talks, and acts like, nor should he have a static idea of how to "make a disciple." No program or person will ever make a disciple. Only God *makes* disciples.

The moment we trust in and rely on programs and strategies, as important as they are, we make our most fatal theological error. The main goal in discipleship is to be Christlike. Only the Spirit can make a disciple; only the Spirit can create Christlikeness in any person. What the Spirit creates will at times not be in accordance with *our* master plan, but if the Spirit does it, then it is superior to our plan.

In the third word picture Jesus assisted Nicodemus by dipping into some Old Testament imagery to illustrate his previous points. The statement is a strange one, particularly to us, but at the same time full of meaning for Nicodemus.

> "No one has ever gone into heaven except the one who came from heaven—the Son of Man." (John 3:13)

"Son of Man" seemed to be Jesus' favorite title for himself. He used it over eighty times. It had certain Messianic connotations to Jewish scholars, implying One sent from heaven who is partly divine, partly human—One who would build a bridge between Israel and God. Nicodemus was immediately aware that Jesus was speaking of One who was from heaven but who was at that time on earth. Then Jesus added the heart of the metaphor, sparking even more cognition in the scholar's mind.

> "Just as Moses lifted up the snake in the desert, so the Son of Man must be lifted up, that everyone who believes in him may have eternal life." (John 3:14-15)

Nicodemus' memory was immediately triggered to recall the incident in Numbers 21 where the venomous snakes bit the Israelites. Moses was told to make a snake of bronze and set it on a pole. Whoever had been bitten could look at the bronze snake and then be healed. Just as the snake was raised up and people were healed, so the Son of Man would be raised up and deliverance would be theirs for the believing. No system of works could replace that sacrifice.

This creative metaphor of the snake demonstrates how Jesus' method of discussing eternal life with someone involved speaking in language that would both capture the person's imagination and enable him to understand. Thus, when he followed up this statement with the gospel thrust of John 3:16, it was more than just words to Nicodemus. For here was a piece of an unsolved puzzle that he had not yet been able to put together. That which he had been seeking for most of his adult life was now his. In this passage we come to see the key to effective, creative evangelism. Often when we speak to others in traditional religious language, they nod their heads, yet do not truly comprehend what is being said. Such communication is ineffective because of our inability or unwillingness to take the time to discover their frame of reference, and our failure to state our message in a creative way.

The final word picture given by Jesus to Nicodemus is one of light and darkness.

> "This is the verdict: Light has come into the world, but men loved darkness instead of light because their deeds were evil. Everyone who does evil hates the light, and will not come into the light for fear that his deeds will be exposed. But whoever lives by the truth comes into the light, so that it may be seen plainly that what he has done has been done through God." (John 3:19-21)

The implication in this illustration is that those who desire to know God will come to the light; all others will remain in darkness. This clearcut contrast was a way of giving Nicodemus the opportunity to make what we refer to as a decision. What a feather in the cap of Jesus if, at this early stage of the campaign, he could win one so influential. What a demonstration to the disciples of the wisdom of Jesus and the spiritual need of Israel's leadership. It is a bit surprising that no decision, yea or nay, is recorded in the text at this point. To some it might be even more amazing that Jesus did not press for one.

Jesus didn't press Nicodemus because he doesn't always desire or require a snap decision. If Nicodemus had chosen Christ, it would have meant an abrupt end to his life as he had known it. His family would have disowned him. And it would have meant not only excommunication from the Sanhedrin and from the party of the Pharisees, but also dismissal from the synagogue itself. Nicodemus would have been an outcast, a traitor. Was he willing to pay such a high price for truth?

Jesus did not want an emotional decision that could not be seriously lived out in the long run. For when someone makes a decision to follow Christ, he is not at the finish line, but at the starting line. There is a long way to go on the road of true discipleship.

Success in evangelism comes only when we follow what God commands; the results are *his* concern, not ours. It is not our responsibility to lead people to Christ. God simply asks us to tell others about Christ, allowing the Holy Spirit to take care of the rest. If we obey God with dedication and creativity in our evangelism attempts, then we are successful in his sight no matter what the results. If, however, we experience no positive results over an extended period of time, we should evaluate our methods and motives.

Staying on course

Knowing where you are going is a requisite for effective leadership. But even after you have decided where you are going, it is important to keep on going—to stay on course. Jesus resisted the attempts of others to hastily crown him king of Israel because his time had not yet come. Even at this early stage of ministry we observe the diligent obedience of Christ to his divine agenda. He knew that he had to remain on the path that was right for him.

There had arisen something of a dispute among John's disciples because Jesus was drawing larger crowds than John. John immediately set his men straight by reminding them of his role, the identity of Jesus, and the blessing of God on his Son (John 3:22-36). John, too, knew the importance of staying on course. His words testify to his spiritual maturity and insight: "[Jesus] must become greater; I must become less" (John 3:30).

When Jesus learned of John's arrest for condemning Herod's adultery, he *withdrew* from the controversial situation by going back into Galilee (John 4:1-3). But why did he retreat from controversy?

Jesus knew that as soon as he forced the issue with the Pharisees, then the tension between himself and Israel's leadership would escalate to a showdown. It would not be long before the Pharisees ran out of smear tactics, and in a back-room meeting they would decide that death would be the only solution. If Jesus' ministry time was to be reduced from three and one-half years to one year, he would have needed to immediately begin teaching his men about the cost of discipleship, the cross, and their own suffering. But these faithful men were not yet ready for such talk. In fact, he waited until only ten months before the Crucifixion to first introduce the concept of the Cross. The disciples were the key to the future, but they were not prepared at this time to be on their own. In this sense, Jesus withdrew to Galilee to keep the disciples on course in their training program.

If you are convinced that your plan of ministry is God's own blueprint, then do not change it just because of external pressure. Often a disciple is tempted to redirect or reschedule the biblical motif because it seems like the natural thing to do. A typical example is a young man who, after giving his life to Christ, hits the ground running, showing great potential for the future. The temptation is to place him in leadership *now*, when in fact to do so would be to violate the biblical emphasis on the importance of thorough discipleship training. We must be careful not to jump the gun in order to get quick, more visible results. The advice and example of Jesus is to wait, have faith, and stick with the plan.

The disciples needed more *time*. There is absolutely no substitute for time when it comes to developing a mature disciple. After the seeds of commitment are planted, they need time to grow. The *"Come and see"* phase is embryonic in the discipleship plan. These men had not even formed the right questions, let alone the right answers. Common sense teaches that people are not willing to die for something they don't believe in. Faith can be stabilized only through the course of time.

The disciples were to be with Jesus only four months during this first phase; then they would go home to allow the seeds of thought to grow into conviction. Subsequently, Jesus would call them into a new phase of exposure and training on a somewhat deeper level—the *"Come and follow me"* phase, which was a ten-month period. They would, at this point, be leaving their professions for nearly a year, a much greater commitment than they had previously been asked to give.

Finally, there was the commitment to give up everything on a permanent basis, including their very lives. This was the third phase of Jesus' training ministry—*"Come and be with me,"* which was a twenty-month time frame during which he prepared them to be able to disciple others. To abort the natural process of these three phases, to deny these faithful men the time to develop into the finished product, would be to eliminate the deep conviction that was necessary to prepare ten of the original twelve to die a martyr's death.

Jesus withdrew for the good of his men and for the future of his Church. A spiritual leader should make decisions based on what is best for those he serves, and for the cause to which he has committed himself.

Evangelizing the forgotten

During the time of Moses, God commanded the people of Israel not to intermarry with those outside the Jewish community. The primary purpose was the protection of Israel's spiritual purity. Adhering to such a command is difficult under normal circumstances, but when the ten northern tribes were overrun by Gentile armies from the massive Assyrian Empire in 722 B.C., obedience became very difficult. As a result, there was much intermarriage, some voluntary, some otherwise. The Jews of the southern kingdom (Judah) considered the offspring of these mixed marriages to be something worse than a Jew or even a Gentile —a half-breed. To the purebred Jew, the half-breeds who lived north of Jerusalem in the region called Samaria were dogs, the scum of the earth, a rotten stench in the nostrils of God. The feeling of disdain was so sharp that when a Jew would travel from Judea to the northern region of Galilee, he would often go far out of his way to travel around Samaria. It is interesting to find that Jesus dispensed with this traditional travel adjustment, heading straight into Samaria on his way to Galilee (John 4:3-42).

After a full morning's journey, Jesus was weary, so he

stopped at a well near the town of Sychar. It was about noon,
and probably it was extremely hot. At this well Jesus met a
thirsty woman and, in addition, offered his disciples a unique
seminar in evangelism. There is a great contrast between
this woman and Nicodemus.

> She was all that Nicodemus was not. He was a Jew; she was a
> Samaritan. He was a man; she was a woman. He was
> learned; she was ignorant. He was morally upright; she was
> sinful. He was wealthy and from the upper class of society;
> she was poor, and probably almost an outcast. He recog-
> nized Jesus' merits and sought Him out; she saw Him only
> as a curious traveler and was quite indifferent to Him.
> Nicodemus was serious and dignified; she was flippant and
> possibly boisterous.[1]

This radical difference in personalities provides us with a
laboratory of learning concerning the adaptation of the
gospel message to people with different frames of reference.

   In the case of this woman at the well, Jesus initiated the
conversation. He was not afflicted with the disease of many
Christians: "evangelistic lock jaw." Jesus had no pressure on
him to perform, and so his relaxed, unforced response to the
lady's presence was simply to start talking and see what
would come of the conversation. Jesus simply asked for a
drink. The lady, being somewhat sassy, said in effect, "Why
would you talk to me? I'm a Samaritan woman and you are a
Jewish man. To the Jews, I'm dirt, the scum of the earth."
Jesus' retort was quick and provocative:

> Jesus answered her, "If you knew the gift of God and who it
> is that asks you for a drink, you would have asked him and
> he would have given you living water."
>   "Sir," the woman said, "you have nothing to draw with
> and the well is deep. Where can you get this living water? Are

you greater than our father Jacob, who gave us the well and
drank from it himself, as did also his sons and his flocks and
herds?"

Jesus answered, "Everyone who drinks this water will be
thirsty again, but whoever drinks the water I give him will
never thirst. Indeed, the water I give him will become in him a
spring of water welling up to eternal life." (John 4:10-14)

Her response to this strange substance called "living
water" was, "Where can I get some? If I could get some, I
wouldn't need to come down here and draw water and be
ridiculed by all those self-righteous gossips." Jesus had
struck a responsive chord. The principle is that he found a
need that he could meet in her life. He understood her
frame of reference. He knew what she hated (coming down
to draw water) and what she needed (a change in her life).
But before he could help her need, he had to pique her
interest.

There are needs pressing in on all people from every
side. As society decays, the economy struggles, which gives
rise to splintered families, unemployment, and financial
disaster. The Church should follow the example of Jesus,
finding out what the needs in our communities are and then
meeting them. This would give us at least part of the key to
the responsive chord in those who are without Christ. But
before we can meet their spiritual need, we must first arouse
their interest. Let us open our eyes to our neighbors, work
colleagues, relatives, and those within our sphere of influence, identifying their needs and attempting to approach
them with the love of Christ. This will make it possible for
them to open up to receive their own deliverance.

Jesus zeroed in on the woman's deepest need when he
told her to go call her husband. She then denied that she was
married. Jesus leveled her with his candid reply. He told her

in so many words, "That's right, you've had five husbands, plus the one you're living with now, that makes six, and he's not even your husband." Her response is priceless: "Sir, I can see that you are a prophet." She knew that somehow this man saw right through her.

Then, feeling somewhat uneasy, she attempted to change the subject. What better way to get the conversation off her needs and on to something else than to bring up an age-old religious controversy. She tried to get Jesus to state his opinion on whether the true place of worship was Jerusalem (the Jewish view) or the appointed place in Samaria on the ground near Jacob's well (the Samaritan view). Jesus answered her diversion by telling her that what is important is not the place of worship but rather the manner of worship, whether or not it is based on truth. He was making a clear distinction here between form and function, a distinction that is desperately needed in the evangelical community.

Jesus let the woman know that he was not interested in getting involved in the factionalism of this religious debate. He was more interested in meeting her need. He would not allow himself to get sidetracked. She finally gave in, admitting her need and interest: "I know that Messiah (called Christ) is coming. When he comes, he will explain everything to us" (4:25). Jesus simply responded, "I who speak to you am he."

When the disciples returned, they must have learned a lot from this episode of the woman. The fact that it was recorded in such great detail by John tells us that Jesus thoroughly described it to his disciples, probably as an evangelistic teaching tool. In the encounter with Nicodemus, we see how Jesus evangelized an already religious man. In the case of the woman at the well, we have a primary example of how the Master approached one who was by no means religious—one of the forgotten ones.

A willingness to break with tradition

When the disciples returned from town, they were "surprised to find that [Jesus] had been talking with a woman" (4:27). It was unusual for a Jewish man, particularly a rabbi, to speak to a woman in public, especially to a Samaritan woman of ill repute. They were flabbergasted, yet not brave enough to say anything about it to Jesus. There is an interesting old rabbinical saying concerning speaking to women: "A man shall not be alone with a woman in an inn, not even with his sister or his daughter, on account of what men may think. A man shall not talk with a woman in the street, not even with his own wife, and especially not with another woman, on account of what men may say."[2]

Here we see that Jesus had once again broken with the accepted tradition. But look at the fantastic results of this breach of the oral law: many people in Samaria were saved due to the testimony of this seemingly insignificant woman (4:28-30, 39-42). Because of his simple encounter with this woman, Jesus was invited to stay several days longer, ministering to the needs of the community, bringing the people the word of salvation. What if he had strictly followed tradition? What if he had been afflicted with "evangelistic lock jaw"? What if he had not been flexible and caring? The answer is grim: the door of ministry to an entire region would have remained closed.

The disciples learned that Jesus would not allow traditional taboos to keep him from reaching out, that there is no such thing as an unclean person who does not deserve to hear the good news. This was demonstrated several times in the ministry of Jesus with the lepers, the blind, the poor, the rich, the demon-possessed, and the children. Yes, even the children were treated as unimportant targets for evangelism by the religious community and the disciples.

We need a certain loving, caring attitude to order to get

through to people. The axiom is true: People do not care how much you know until they know how much you care. The applications of this principle for twentieth century Christians are numerous. We must not allow prejudices and traditional taboos to stand in the way of reaching people for Christ. This we can know for sure: if we do allow race, economic status, or social status to impede the Great Commission, then we are clearly out of God's will.

Up to this point, before they arrived there at the well that day, the disciples probably had many unasked questions formed in their minds about what made Jesus tick: What is he really after? What is the bottom line in evangelism? He doesn't seem to want to be crowned king or to conquer the Romans. What does he have in mind?

There at Jacob's well Jesus revealed the driving force within him. As usual, the Master built his teaching on an ordinary situation. The disciples knew that Jesus was hot and hungry, for it had been several hours since they had eaten. They offered him food, but we are given the impression that he refused it. Then he made a statement that was both profound and puzzling. "I have food to eat that you know nothing about" (4:32). The disciples were perplexed, and so they conversed among themselves in a vain attempt to understand what he was talking about. But Jesus soon stopped them by explaining, "My food is to do the will of him who sent me and to finish his work."

Jesus likened doing the will of the Father to eating. It is a biological fact that food is necessary to health, growth, and even survival. Eating is a habit that is exceedingly difficult to break, one to which I have been enslaved all my earthly life. My taste buds are aroused at the mere mention of certain culinary delights. The anticipation of joy as that favorite dish is set on the table piping hot is pleasant torture.

Food is exceedingly enjoyable to most of us. Could

doing the will of God be just as exciting? Jesus indicated that both the enjoyment of and the nourishment provided by doing the will of the Father were as important to him as food. Think of it! To do God's will is as much of a necessity in our lives as our need to eat! Jesus was saying in effect, What really makes me tick, what keeps me up at night, what is more important than food itself, is pleasing my Father.

I believe there is a positive residual aspect in obeying God, just as there is a positive return in eating. As we learn the benefits of obedience, God begins to bless our lives. We should anticipate doing his will as a positive task that we not only enjoy, but also need. We receive a spiritual nourishment from God that we should perpetually crave.

Jesus thus communicated to his disciples the key to the vitality of his existence. And then he went on to describe the task before *them*: "Do you not say, 'Four months more and then the harvest'? I tell you, open your eyes and look at the fields! They are ripe for harvest" (4:35). There was a spiritual harvest right in front of them, even there in Samaria. There was no need to wait. Evangelism was opportune anytime, any place.

Here was the task defined, the mission before them. The people were there; all that was needed now was a small army of laborers. Jesus had timed it perfectly. The accumulation of all the data and experiences now started coming together like the pieces of a giant jigsaw puzzle. This was what Jesus wanted the disciples to ponder as they went back home to consider what they would do with their lives. It was a tremendous challenge: harvesting men and women for the kingdom of God.

Although Jesus emphasized the urgency of the task of laboring for God, the disciples probably considered certain urgent business back home as well. They had been away now for four months. But the time was coming for them to address a compelling spiritual question: Which is more important—my occupation of fishing or answering the call to harvest? Do I want to live out of a suitcase, spending most of my time away from family and friends, to minister to strangers? Should I go back to a life of tradition, or should I join this holy man who challenges the dead weight of tradition? These are the questions that troubled the freshly initiated men as Jesus sent them back to their more mundane existence.

The determination that this was the end of the "Come and see" phase of Christ's ministry is based on the observation that there is no mention of his disciples during a recorded visit to his hometown in John 4:43-54, Luke 4:16-20, and Matthew 4:13-16. This period was probably one of only a few weeks duration. The next reference to his disciples is found in Matthew 4:18-22 and Mark 1:16-20, at least two months later. Therefore, this brief period of personal soul-searching for the disciples was planned by Christ for the growth of conviction and courage.

As the disciples went home to think things over and straighten out their personal affairs, it was impossible for them to get Jesus out of their minds. The vivid image of ripe harvest fields had shaken them loose from their moorings. The challenge of harvesting men and women for God's kingdom was all the more stimulating when they weighed it in their minds against the common drudgery of harvesting fish.

Jesus wanted to give these men time to allow the seeds he had planted to settle in their souls. This was one of his most effective methods of ensuring the right selection of men. He gave them time to pray and think over the call to discipleship—the invitation to a radical investment of time and effort. As they were out in their fishing boats for hours on end, there was an abundance of time to think. The flashbacks were probably numerous. Perhaps the reserved Andrew reflected back to another modest fellow named Nicodemus. The brazen disciple Peter might have fondly recalled the bold act of clearing the temple, or the time when he was given the name "the Rock." The others might have thought back with wonderment to the phenomenon of water turning into wine.

Envision them as they gathered around the dinner table each evening to share a meal and the day's thoughts. The conversation would eventually find its way to some story about what Jesus did or said. These men were hopelessly hooked. They found this Galilean carpenter irresistible. Indeed, they had the same fixation that two of them would express to the Jewish authorities some years later: "We cannot help speaking about what we have seen and heard" (Acts 4:20).

Every day became a grind as they went about the routine tasks of workingmen. They had never felt this way before. They had always enjoyed their work and found it fulfilling. But now the fish began to stink, the mending of nets seemed trivial, the hours in the boats became unbearable, and they found their minds traveling back to a discussion around a camp fire or a Bible study in a boat. They began to experience what Spurgeon spoke about in his lectures to his students: If you can be happy doing anything other than preaching, by all means do it. But if all else apart from this holy task blurs into insignificance, then respond to the call.

Footnotes:
1. Tenney, *John*, page 92.
2. H. L. Strack and P. Billerbeck, *Kommentar zum Neuen Testament aus Talmud und Midrasch,* (Munchen, Volume 2, 1922-28), page 438.

PRINCIPLES AND SUGGESTIONS

1. *Choose people as your method.* Jesus' ministry centered around the training and building of disciples. He chose disciples who were teachable, curious, and interested in serving God. You should follow the Master's example by choosing the ripe and ready people to disciple.

2. *Help potential converts to make solid decisions.* Do not exploit others' weaknesses in order to accomplish a goal. Discipling is a long-range enterprise, demanding solid, thought-out decisions. Plan to allow people the time and information they need, thus ensuring that decisions are made during a time of clear-headedness and emotional balance.

3. *Recognize your place in ministry and then stay there.* When

you exercise your gifts faithfully, you always meet needs. You should never try to evade your calling by going off into some other ministry for variety or escape.

4. *Give your disciples an initial taste for ministry.* Without choking them on too much too soon, you should expose your disciples gradually to the nature of Christian ministry, both the bitter and the sweet. Assign limited tasks for them to do, giving them a taste for success and a hunger for more.

5. *Give disciples a vision for what they can become.* Look for the positive qualities in converts, the potentialities that can be shaped by God into maturity. Be on the lookout to find and encourage people in the early stages of their spiritual pilgrimage, when they are looking for handles and helps in that journey.

6. *Make it easy for them to say no.* Make sure that your candidates for discipleship know what they are getting into. Do not use pressure techniques or shortcuts in order to get quick commitments. Instead, take the pressure off yourself and the recruit by making it easy for him to say no to your invitation.

7. *Motivate your disciples by the indirect method of modeling.* Everything we do teaches, whether we like it or not. The deepest impression we leave on others is the one that naturally flows out of our daily living rather than our carefully planned prototype. If you are not willing to get truly close to a few people for Christ, then you will not have the full impact that is vital in discipleship.

8. *Identify the spiritual enemy.* On various occasions, Jesus exposed the devices of Satan, our spiritual enemy. A discipler should always be discerning and honest enough to point out to his disciples the negative elements that stand as obstacles in our spiritual pathway. Help your disciples see the nature of spiritual warfare.

9. *Use a "tailor-made" approach in witnessing.* Because

each person you encounter is different, your evangelistic approach needs to be flexible and creative. Take the time to establish a "frame of reference" with each person, speaking in familiar language. It is vitally important to be familiar with at least one way of introducing others to Christ, but be sensitive enough to tailor your approach to the personal characteristics of others.

10. *Do not allow prejudice to stand in the path of ministry.* Jesus broke with traditional taboos in order to meet the need of the Samaritan woman. Any discrimination on our part that would keep us from obedience to God is sinful and counter-productive to our spiritual lives. We should follow the practice of Christ by exposing our disciples to others different from themselves.

11. *Demonstrate that you know where you are going.* One sure sign of successful leadership is that the person in charge understands the plan and communicates it to those he wishes to enlist in the enterprise. Jesus demonstrated a resolute plan for the enlisting, training, and spiritual reproduction of disciples. He explained to his men that his food was to do the will of his Father.

12. *Recognize the importance of timing in your ministry.* A good leader has a sense of timing in his own ministry, taking into account the long run. He is also sensitive to the right timing for his disciples. God's plan and our corresponding agenda should never be slave to the world's calendar or clock.

13. *Challenge your disciples to share in your vision.* After the proper preparation had been made, Jesus clearly laid before his men the task at hand. His vision was the harvesting of the souls of lost people. After an introductory exposure to the nature of ministry, your disciples are ready for a challenge. If they are adequately prepared, your challenge will make sense and hopefully set their prepared hearts aflame.

14. *Give them time to make a solid decision.* After you call your disciples to ministry, give them time to make their decision. Review with them the commitment, and then give them several days to think it over. After they have been exposed to the first twelve principles in this section, challenge them to invest their lives in a more permanent training arrangement. But then give them some time and space.

Part 2

COME AND FOLLOW ME:
Establishing

As Jesus walked beside the Sea of Galilee, he saw
Simon and his brother Andrew casting a net into
the lake, for they were fishermen. "Come, follow
me," Jesus said, "and I will make you fishers of
men." At once they left their nets and followed
him.

   When he had gone a little farther, he saw
James son of Zebedee and his brother John in a
boat, preparing their nets. Without delay he called
them, and they left their father Zebedee in the
boat with the hired men and followed him.

Mark 1:16-20

4
THE TASTE OF NEW WINE

When the disciples left Jesus to return to their fishing, they were faced with a contrast between two totally different worlds. Here they were, back at their nets, with visions of the Messiah swimming about in their minds. Jesus left each of these men thinking, praying, and struggling with the question, "Should I follow him?" They were not sure when the decision would come, but they knew that some day they must choose. To live for the world *or* to live for Jesus—it was a clear-cut choice.

The incentive to fish for men
It is incredible that a person would drop the baggage of the world to follow Jesus, considering the present competition for our time. Civic organizations, work-related functions, political groups, various lodges and orders, thousands of

committees and programs—all of them vie for the bits and pieces of our available time. Because there are so many roads we can and do travel, we can see the compelling nature of the call facing the early disciples: giving up a lot of relatively worthy options to focus on a singular, emphatic life-commitment. Why would anyone be willing to put everything on the line like this?

However, I find even more astonishing Jesus' choice of personnel to reach the world: not men of means, an elite strata of society, or men of the ecclesiastical establishment, but simple Galilean fishermen, rough and somewhat pedestrian in their thinking, influenced by Jewish passions and prejudices. They were slow to learn and slower still to unlearn. Why would such practical, hardworking, down-to-earth men want to risk it all to pursue an unknown quest?

When we consider all of the factors deterring the disciples from pursuing a ministry with Jesus, the following account takes on a more special significance:

> As Jesus walked beside the Sea of Galilee, he saw Simon and his brother Andrew casting a net into the lake, for they were fishermen. "Come, follow me," Jesus said, "and I will make you fishers of men." At once they left their nets and followed him.
>
> When he had gone a little farther, he saw James son of Zebedee and his brother John in a boat, preparing their nets. Without delay he called them, and they left their father Zebedee in the boat with the hired men and followed him. (Mark 1:16-20)

The fishermen instantly dropping their nets to follow Jesus causes the salesman to drool, the politician to turn green with envy, and the psychologist to scratch his head.

Why did they *immediately* drop their nets and follow

Christ? Some think Jesus, being God, had a special power over them, that he cast a spell or hypnotized his followers and that, therefore, they were not free moral agents. Intriguing as this may sound, I think the motive for following Jesus in this case was far more simple: these men followed Jesus at his bidding because *they had already been with him.*

A chronological review of the disciples' exposure to Jesus reveals that during the initial four-month "Come and see" period, they received an intensive exposure to Jesus and to the nature of ministry. During this period, these men experienced life-changing discussions with Jesus. They saw him perform miracles, clear the temple, witness to both a religious leader and an immoral woman, and challenge the religious establishment. To these orthodox conservatives, these men who had seen their fill of fish and of religious hypocrisy, this was the taste of new wine.

The men had gone home to think it over, to allow time for digestion of what had taken place. They were probably not even aware of how long it had been. (It was around two or three months.)[1] There had been time to straighten out personal affairs, and time to allow the seeds that Jesus had planted to grow into solid conviction. The seeds grew and conviction came. For, when the day of decision was upon them, they left everything and followed him.

A principle repeated often in the life of Jesus is, *Give people time to make solid decisions.* Jesus didn't rush his men. Consequently, like ripe fruit ready for picking, when the time came they offered no resistance.

Another reason why these men immediately followed Christ is that *they were given an invitation, not a responsibility.* "Follow me" is a simple invitation. What is even more impressive than what Jesus said is what he didn't say. He didn't say, "Follow me and I will make you leaders and preachers." Nor did he say, "Peter, the future of the Church rests in your hands; you will give the inaugural message for the Church. Furthermore, you will take your place as the first Pope." Nor did he say, "John, you will be imprisoned and persecuted greatly for my sake." He didn't give them enticing promises or specific prophecies because he knew in his wisdom that these men were not prepared. Jesus understood the hearts of men (John 2:24), and so he knew the disciples' tolerance level for new information. Therefore, even as late as the eve of his Crucifixion (John 16:12), Jesus withheld certain information from them because he knew what they could not endure or understand.

I have disregarded this principle several times in my own life, and have witnessed regretful results. Once, after leading someone to Christ, I was inclined to tell him everything that stimulated and motivated me. I told this new convert of his vast potential for pastoring or missionary work, and added that, if he really got lucky, he might even suffer for the cause. Later, when I could not find my new disciple, I naturally assumed the devil had gotten him. But the devil didn't get him; I did! I overwhelmed him with information he was not ready to bear.

The news that we are destined for Christian leadership is not good news unless God's Spirit has prepared us. The most expensive real estate in the New Testament, the passages that speak of his coming suffering, are found only in the last ten months of Jesus' ministry.

The Master gives a simple invitation—no hard-line ultimatums, no forced behavior. If you want to come along, now is the time; or, you also have the opportunity to say no. Jesus makes it easy to say no. He doesn't want any rash decisions.

Jesus assumed full responsibility: "Follow me and *I* will make you. . . ." He would bear the weight of their training. He would not ask of them anything that he himself had not shown them. When a convert joins a discipleship group, it should be on the basis of a simple invitation, with the knowledge that the group leader takes the responsibility to train him. The responsibility of the convert in becoming a disciple is simply to respond to the invitation of Christ and to allow God's Spirit, via the human instrument (a Christian leader), to train him. The discipler's task, then, is to increase the convert's appetite for the work of ministry through selective exposure. For example, the discipler should expose the new recruit to positive evangelism experiences to breed confidence and yet show him his need for more training.

This type of show-and-tell training could be likened to taking a group to the beach on a beautiful day. Some would immediately jump off the bus, shed their gear as they sprinted toward the beach, and do a somersault into the surf. Some would sunbathe; others would go for a walk; and a few would possibly remain in street clothes, not venturing near the water. If the leader's goal is to get this entire group into the water, he will need to make more than one trip to the beach. He will need to return again and again. The leader himself should lead the charge, willing to be the first one to get wet. He will keep taking his converts back to the beach until all join in and enjoy the experience. The discipler will keep exposing his trainees to positive evangelistic experiences until even the most hesitant will begin to feel comfortable.

Jesus' primary method of changing the disciples from fishers of fish to fishers of men was to expose them again and again to ministry opportunities that he initiated and modeled for them. It is a serious mistake to send a boy out to do a man's job. It is just as problematic to send an untrained convert out to do a trained disciple's task.

I once told a young man how to use an evangelistic tool. The key word is *told*; I didn't model it. He was confident that he would be able to do what I told him. We approached a

man, and the young man introduced the evangelistic tool
into the conversation. All was well for a sentence or two until
the man asked a couple of questions concerning the booklet
itself that my protégé could not answer. He not only had no
answers; he was dumbfounded! Through this very experience the lad lost interest in ministry.

My disappointment, the man's aborted opportunity to
hear the gospel clearly, and my trainee's disillusionment
were all unnecessary, all because I had failed to heed this
simple rule: Never ask someone to do something you have
not trained him to do. The training begins with our modeling the process itself. My trainee did not know what to do
because I had failed to model witnessing. If only I had done
so, then he would have had a guarded opportunity to learn
without taking on the responsibility, and thus he would have
been stimulated to learn more.

The disciples dropped everything to follow Jesus because they had previously been with him and because he
gave them an invitation, not a responsibility. Without the
previous exposure there would have been no solid interest;
without the invitation they would have stayed where they
were. There is one more reason why they followed; without
it the disciples would have considered the call boring.

Jesus called them to a vision, not to a job. A disillusioned
executive once lamented concerning his career, "I have
learned much in the last forty years; unfortunately, most of it
is about aluminum." Nearly anyone can hold a job; precious
few can live for a dream. One of man's greatest fears is that
his life will not count, that he will look back at his investment
of time and effort only to conclude that it was a waste. Men's
hearts are not set aflame by the mundane. People are not
motivated by the prospect of building a monument to medi-
ocrity. "Where there is no vision, the people perish" (Proverbs 29:18, KJV).

There is no danger that Jesus would allow his followers to perish for a lack of meaning. When Jesus calls a person, he calls him to a purpose, a dream, a goal, a life-changing vision. The vision is to be a fisher of men. These Galilean men understood fishing, and they were certainly acquainted with the lost state of men. Therefore, the call to fish for men turned their heads; their hearts were aflame for it!

There is nothing quite as exhilarating as getting out of bed in the morning, going back into the world, and knowing why. Enthusiasm is derived from the certainty that for this I was born, and I am doing it! It is the thrilling knowledge that I am fulfilling God's intended purpose for me.

There is nothing quite as debilitating as having one's vision eroded and spirit smashed somehow by a certain kind of exposure to God's calling. The birth of a vision in ministry can often lead to the death of a vision because of the very work itself. Many enthusiastic believers have plunged head-first into ministry, only to leave it later, bitter and critical. This is one explanation of why there are so few fishers of men. But how does it happen?

Jesus warned us about the insidious nature of *leaven* (the spiritual yeast of sin) working its way into our lives. The four leavens in Scripture are hypocrisy (Matthew 16, 23), rationalization (Matthew 16, 23), impurity (1 Corinthians 5), and legalism (Galatians 5). These are vision killers. They will take the enthusiasm right out of believers, thus gradually sapping the heart out of ministry. When the work of the Church becomes just church work, when the work of ministry becomes simply a job rather than a vision, then it is time to reevaluate what is going on.

This distinction between positive and negative perspectives can be seen in the story of two boys describing the work of their fathers. Both fathers were riveters in an airplane factory. The first boy said, "Oh, my father is just a riveter."

The second boy said proudly, "My dad builds airplanes!" Apparently the one father just had a job, but the other possessed a vision.

When people lose vision for ministry, the work becomes cold, hard, and cruel. It is frightening how easily we can be duped by the devil into majoring on the minors, creating strife by our nitpicking, and becoming immersed in detail. Every day that this unholy diversion continues, our vision slowly dies.

My grandfather used to keep hunting dogs in a large pen in our back yard. During the hunting season, the dogs would be docile in their pen, getting along rather well. During the times of the year when there was no hunting, they would become irritable, continually fighting among themselves. The reason was simple: they were hunting dogs, and so they were meant to hunt. When they were not able to hunt, they found other, more unproductive activities. A critical Christian who has lost his vision for the work of ministry will eventually depart from the dream or goal of the Church.

I have found that the closer a person is to a critical spirit, the further away he will be from personal evangelism. I cannot name one faultfinding Christian who shares his faith on a regular basis. Constant criticism is destructive to one's spiritual health.

We must be on guard to keep our vision alive and in good health. In 1963 Martin Luther King stood in the shadow of the Lincoln Memorial in Washington, D.C. and spoke the words, "I have a dream!" It was that dream that sustained him and brought greater freedom for blacks. Jesus, too, had a dream, and by his method of recruitment he spread this dream to a handful of others who were willing to become fishers of men.

Jesus is calling millions to follow him into the harvest fields to become disciples, learning how to labor. He wants to recruit those who are certain they want to be there. Being a disciple is a long-term commitment. It requires serious training. A sincere disciple of Jesus must become *established* in Bible study, prayer, fellowship, and witnessing. Being established means that hearing, reading, studying, meditating, and memorizing God's word become a natural part of everyday life.

Encouragement, exhortation, comforting, and accountability will be present in their fellowship, along with a balanced social life. They will be sharing their faith as a way of life, participating in the witnessing opportunities that God gives them. Finally, they will be willing to allow a leader to see to it that these qualities of a disciple are being properly developed in their lives.

When the potential disciple is called out to ministry, it is important for the leader to take on the responsibility of training him, making sure that he is not put in situations he is not equipped to handle. And always the vision must be kept before him, reminding him of the reason why he is fishing for men.

He showed them how
Jesus had a handful of men who were now prepared to learn from the Master. They were watching closer and taking mental notes because, for the first time, they could see themselves doing the same kind of ministries someday. Jesus' methods are difficult to outline or place into a manual. He blended ministry skills with character development, teaching his protégés by example in the laboratory of life. Jesus did not declare, "Men, we will now learn!" Announcing that class is in session often impedes the learning process. We learn best when we are unaware that learning is taking place. He didn't tell his men to spread out and witness; rather, they were simply to watch him.

When Jesus entered the synagogue in Capernaum, he immediately began to teach (Mark 1:21). This was effective strategy, for the synagogue provided him with a forum to teach. This synagogue ministry was particularly strategic in reaching "the lost sheep" of the house of Israel, which was at the top of God's "do list."

The normal order of service in the synagogue was praise to God, then a prayer, followed by a Scripture reading, and crowned with an exposition of Scripture. Traditionally, if any theologically competent person such as a rabbi was present, he would be invited to give the exposition of Scripture. Jesus was accepted in this capacity because he already had a reputation among the Jews as an authoritative and challenging teacher.

The first indication that Jesus struck a nerve of need is in verse 22: "The people were amazed at his teaching, because he taught them as one who had authority." The people were thunderstruck. The teaching of Jesus had a way of moving people outside of their mundane world, giving them sight of a better kingdom and a taste of new wine. The Master's teaching was not dry, dead, and hard to understand like the typical messages from the rabbinical pulpit. It wasn't just another boring homily by a pseudo-theologian trying to impress other pseudo-theologians. It was a message that stirred the hearts of people.

Joseph Parker, a nineteenth-century preacher said, "If you preach to hurting hearts, you will never want for a congregation; there is one in every pew." The effect in the Capernaum synagogue was that the word of God gripped the hearts of people. It was an enlightening exposition.

Among those who were on the edge of their pews, absorbing every word, were the disciples. They had heard Jesus teach the Scripture before with power when they first met. But now they found themselves drinking in the word of

God as members of his team. When Jesus taught the Scripture, the hearts of those who listened burned within them (Luke 24:32).

Jesus emphasized early in his ministry the power of the Scriptures and the necessity of knowing them. Jewish men believed in the supernatural nature of Scripture, but few had experienced more than an academic interaction with them. Christ desired something more than a mere exercise of the mind. He wanted people to witness the power and relevance of God's word for themselves. As the writer of Hebrews states, "The word of God is living and active. Sharper than any double-edged sword, it penetrates even to dividing soul and spirit, joints and marrow; it judges the thoughts and attitudes of the heart" (Hebrews 4:12). Listening to, reading, studying, meditating on, memorizing, and applying the word of God should be a soul-stirring process.

Jesus had begun to school the disciples in the fundamentals. The basis of all their spiritual education began during this ten-month training period, this "Come and follow me" phase. The Master had to be sure that the word, prayer, fellowship, and witnessing were rooted deeply in their experience. The surest way to whet their appetites for accomplishing these disciplines was to let them see them in action.

I devoted sixteen years of my life to the game of basketball. As a boy of ten I was motivated by the great collegiate and professional players. I saw in them what I wanted to be, and so I set out to model my life after theirs. I began by mastering the fundamentals: dribbling, passing, shooting, rebounding. Fifteen years later I was playing on a team composed of former collegiate stars, players who had established themselves as some of the best basketball players in the country. What does an accomplished group such as this practice every day? The fundamentals: dribbling, passing,

shooting, rebounding. Regardless of how great a player
becomes, he must still diligently practice the fundamentals,
because they are the foundation of his game. The moment
he abandons sound fundamentals, his game begins to de-
teriorate.

The Christian must be established in these four fundamentals: the word, prayer, fellowship, and witnessing.
Whatever he becomes in later life, regardless of the skills he
acquires, he will be only as strong as he is in the fundamentals. This never changes; there is no other way to become a
consistent disciple.

While Jesus was teaching there in the synagogue, a man
who possessed an evil spirit cried out, "What do you want
with us, Jesus of Nazareth? Have you come to destroy us? I
know who you are—the Holy One of God!" (Mark 1:24).
The disciples knew that Jesus was an eloquent orator who
ministered the word of God with power, but could he handle
a pack of demons? (The man with the unclean spirit introduced himself as "we," meaning several.) Here was a unique
test of Jesus' authority. But it is noteworthy that the forces of
evil did not argue the deity and authority of Christ. They
accepted his authority and begged to be left alone.

Jesus rebuked the spirits and they came out of the man
"with a shriek." The man was relieved at last, and the on-
lookers were astounded. They had been amazed at his profound, authoritative teaching (verse 22), and now they were
amazed to the extent of alarm or fear (verse 27). They
challenged each other to explain what had taken place.
"What is this? A new teaching—and with authority!" There
is a bit of humor here. New teaching they were used to. But
with authority to back it up—that was something to be dealt
with. Human nature, being what it is, can tolerate almost any
new idea as long as it doesn't demand a decision or change.
But anyone who could keep a synogogue crowd awake,

indeed spellbound, and cause demons to come out of a madman, could not be ignored.

The news about Jesus spread instantaneously throughout the entire region. He didn't need a press agent to extol his ability because his work spoke for itself. True authority never needs to toot its own horn. The spiritually-minded recognize such reality. This man's works substantiated his words. Implanted in the disciples' minds was the authenticity and value of God's word. Only when a man sees proof that God's written word works will he dedicate himself to the study and application of it. Jesus spoke from familiar Scriptures in the synagogue, and yet the people were amazed as if they were hearing them for the first time. As they saw him cast the unclean spirits from the madman, their astonishment was advanced to maximum dimensions. The hearing and the testing of God's word proved its value and power beyond their wildest expectations.

Witnessing (declaring the gospel to unbelievers) is a valuable and rewarding experience. If a Christian knows this fact but does not practice it, it is nothing more than theory. I can tell you that chocolate ice-cream is delicious. I can use my powers of persuasion, and even convince you of what I say. But until you actually taste chocolate ice-cream, you do not really *know*. Many Christians don't witness because they realize it is important in their minds but lack a heartfelt knowledge of its value. Their knowledge is intellectual, but not empirical.

The Bible is a frustrating, guilt-producing document if its principles are not practiced by the reader. Jesus saw to it that his men would not be guilty, defeated disciples. He took them into the classroom of spiritual reality and made it come to life. When the disciples at last experienced the *reality* of God's word, they gained convictions that stayed with them all their days.

Mark tells us that Jesus went directly from the synagogue to Simon Peter's house, where Simon's mother-in-law was in bed with a rather serious fever (Mark 1:29-31). Jesus was confronted with this fact as he entered the front door. Just as he was helping her up from her bed, her sickness was gone. Her immediate response was to head for the kitchen to fix something for Jesus, her sons, and the other men.

Many older women will confide in a counseling session something like this: "My children are grown; my husband is retired; I'm struggling with an arthritic condition; I can no longer cook and keep the house up like I used to; I have lost all purpose and dignity." Jesus was never too busy as a discipler to take notice of other people. A discipler's temptation is to be so busy making his life count as he reaches out to the world that he walks past pressing needs. Jesus didn't meet every need; he didn't heal everyone. But he did have a balanced approach to human need.

That evening the needy people started gathering at the entrance of the house. A seemingly endless stream of the physically and spiritually infirm jockeyed for position. The Physician healed many, spending hours ministering to the sick and the wild-eyed. People flock to the place where their needs are met. Because Jesus met needs, he never lacked a following.

As usual, he commanded the demons to keep quiet about his identity (verse 34). This divine gag-order afforded Jesus the time needed to develop a solid ministry. Otherwise, his escalating fame would have forced the religious establishment's hand much too early. Furthermore, his disciples were not yet mature enough to operate without him.

Jesus was approaching the zenith of popularity. Thousands were clamoring for his attention. "Jesus for king" was not an absurdity, but was a viable option for him at this juncture. And yet Jesus would not allow himself to be swept away by the bandwagon mentality, allowing some wayward momentum to carry him to Israel's throne.

Jesus' response to popularity is surprising. The crowds were growing, the needs were pressing in on every side, the opportunities for self-aggrandizement were in abundance. But what did Jesus do at the very peak of this public demand, while the crowds were virtually chanting out his name? "Very early in the morning, while it was still dark, Jesus got up, left the house and went off to a solitary place, where he prayed" (Mark 1:35).

This act of simple devotion is brimming with lessons on how to live with a purpose. Why would Jesus, who was God incarnate, feel a need to pray when everything was going so well? This was no time to pray; there was much work to be done! However, Jesus meant to please his father; he had a very pressing need to speak with him. The Master longed for the perfect fellowship known only to the Godhead.

Prayer was Jesus' way of being nourished. He had given much of himself in recent days, and so he probably needed to recharge his energy. "Come apart or you will come apart," as the axiom goes. Jesus knew that he would be far more useful if he were spiritually healthy. Our Lord did not have a "Messianic complex" or some misguided notion that he had to be busy helping others every waking moment.

It is critical to the success of ministry that we be *balanced* believers, that the ratio of taking in and giving out complement one another. Jesus could have totally occupied himself with sleeping, eating, healing, preaching, and counseling. But the Lord knew that even he needed that additional dimension of *prayer*. He chose to pray because he knew that it was spiritually essential.

Peter and the others were out searching desperately for Jesus. When they finally found him serenely meditating in prayer, they emphatically told him, "Everyone is looking for you!" (Mark 1:37). Their presumptuous implication was, "What are you doing here wasting time praying? There are needy people out there!" These restless, green disciples were not yet aware that activity is not always the answer to success. Pressing needs don't always take precedence over preparation for meeting those same needs. Talking to God is prerequisite to talking to men about God.

Jesus was teaching his men, through his own example, that prayer is foundational to ministry. Prayer and Bible study form two of four pillars of Christian life. As Jesus demonstrated both the authority of Scripture and the priority of prayer, the minds of his harried disciples were being engraved by their Master's poignant demonstration of personal devotion to his Father.

Perhaps accusations were made against Jesus that he was cold, aloof, and interested only in his own agenda. I can hear them now: "All those needy people: how can you turn your back on them? Don't you care?" In a sense, Jesus did turn his back to human need, *but* he simultaneously turned toward the Father's agenda, which, in the long run, was to meet more and deeper needs. He went on to explain his thinking rather succinctly to his disciples: "Let us go somewhere else—to the nearby villages—so I can preach there also. That is why I have come" (1:38).

Christian leaders are often confronted with no-win situations similar to the one Jesus faced here. They are no-win in that if you answer the pressing, immediate human need, then the long-range goal may be neglected. Regardless of the decision, someone is disappointed and some plans are frustrated. The leader is engaged in a constant battle regarding the use of his time. Ultimately, only the leader himself can decide how to use the gifts, abilities, and time God has given him. The agony of this type of decision is shared by every caring leader.

A leader should usually choose the option that will, in the long run, reach the most people with the message of eternal life. This is why discipleship is ordained of God: because its design is to multiply through people the good news to the entire world. This is the essence of the Great Commission. Only those experienced in ministry understand the tension in making such a difficult decision. Verses 38 and 39 reveal that, although Jesus continued to heal and cast out demons, the primary focus of his ministry was the more foundational preaching of the gospel. He had the large picture in mind.

Jesus was not swept away by public opinion. Rather, he chose the unpopular route, the one with the greatest resistance. The action that, in the final analysis, reaches the most people for God, regardless of its appearance, is the most loving, compassionate act of all. When a leader makes this type of decision, he must expect to be criticized.

Because few Christians have a biblical frame of reference for ministry, they consequently assume that love is best demonstrated by meeting the most pressing visible need. Pastors, for example, are constantly engaged in a struggle for time. I often wonder, Should I work on my message two extra hours or visit a shut-in? Teach Bible study leaders or go to a luncheon? Regardless of what I do, someone is going to be unhappy. What is necessary, then, is for the pastor, Christian leader, or discipler to have a simple four-step plan for decision-making.

First, set goals that are scripturally based. Second, set priorities for the activities that are necessary to reach those goals. Third, develop a schedule that reflects your goals and priorities. Fourth, discipline yourself to keep your schedule, which reflects your priorities, which will enable you to achieve your goals. The foremost Achilles heel is discipline, or the lack of it. Without discipline we are like the locomotive fired up to go but with no tracks on which to run. We churn our energy away as we dig deeper into the ground.

If we are to survive the pressures of decision-making, we must, like Jesus, have a clear-cut agenda that we are willing to follow at all costs. There is, however, room for flexibility. There are special situations where a need is so pressing that it cannot be denied.

From catching fish to catching men, the initial sojourn around the Sea of Galilee was brief for Jesus and his fledgling disciples. But the Master crowded much learning into a little time. He demonstrated the authority of Scripture as a wellspring of truth and a foundation for ministry. He taught the high priority of prayer, as evidenced in how he chose to use his time. Outreach of the gospel to needy souls was number one on the Father's agenda.

A message from God (Scripture), a dialogue with God (prayer), and a message to others about God (witnessing)— the importance of these three spiritual fundamentals were gradually established in the lives of the disciples through the loving instruction of the Master. It was his strong desire to extend a full taste of this new wine to all who thirst for eternal life.

Footnotes:
1. Gundry and Thomas, *A Harmony of the Gospels* (Chicago: Moody Press, 1978). My estimate is based partially on the outline and the time line in this book.

5
CONFIRMATION OF THE CALL

When Jesus called the handful of Galilean fishermen away from their nets to follow him, they responded directly to that invitation (Mark 1:16-20). But after a short sojourn with the Master in Capernaum and some surrounding villages (Mark 1:21-39, Luke 4:31-44), the men returned to the Galilean Sea to take up their nets once again (Luke 5:1-11).

Apparently they went home under the guise of straightening up their personal affairs, but Jesus knew better. He knew that they needed a little more time to solidify their commitment, one more time-out from ministry to fish for a few days, experiencing the futility of empty nets.

After an entire night of fishing without a single catch, the disciples were exhausted, and thus ripe for an object lesson from the Master. Jesus had just finished preaching from Peter's fishing boat, and then he turned to the bold disciple and directed him to embark into deep water for a fishing excursion. Peter had just been washing the nets and now the Master was asking him to cast them back down in the water again!

It is interesting to note that Peter didn't mind Jesus *preaching* from his boat; he just didn't like the Master interfering with the business of *fishing* there in his boat (Luke 5:4-5). After all, this was *his* profession. He was a veteran fisherman, convinced that the conditions were not right to go out into deep water as Jesus suggested. Perhaps Peter felt like telling Jesus to stick to preaching.

Would the rookie disciple obey his Master even when it didn't make sense? What would happen if the nets came up empty? Peter would be the laughing stock of the region. Was he willing to be made a fool for Christ?

Disciples come to this place many times over as they attempt to walk with Christ. Jesus seems to keep flinging challenges in our paths, asking us to believe *him* in order to meet those challenges. It was quite a test of Peter's faith to cast those nets. Peter passed the test as he agreed to launch out in faith. The result, of course, was a net-breaking load.

Peter's response to this miracle was utter humiliation. As the nets became overburdened with a record catch, he fell at Jesus' feet and cried out, "Go away from me, Lord; I am a sinful man!" (5:8). This was the response of a guilty man, one who was fighting serious doubt. Peter had been ready to drop out and Jesus knew it. But now Peter realized how foolish he had been to doubt his Master. He had seen Jesus' power before, but this time the Master broke through in a new way. For there in that boat the power of God was made real in Peter's chosen field of endeavor.

What happened in Peter's life happens to many different people in various areas of life. A businessman may attend church for years—faithful in attendance, diligent to serve whenever called upon, and generous with his material treasure—and yet somehow he fails to experience the reality of Christ in his business. Then difficult times put pressure on his marketplace existence, and so he comes up with a novel idea: pray! As in the case of Peter, when God comes through for *you*, it is like experiencing him in a way you never expected. When this kind of liberating experience takes place, you can gain confidence to commit *everything* to Christ. Only when you place all areas of your life in his hands can the abundant life begin.

The disciples were now empirically aware of the importance of Jesus in their lives. Only with *his* help could they really succeed, whether in fishing or some other profession. But why would Jesus want to stay around and help them successfully fish for fish when he was calling them to fish for men? This was the crux of the matter.

Peter's cry of anguish touched Jesus' heart. He knew that his disciple was sincerely repentant, and so he reassured Peter by saying, "Don't be afraid; from now on you will catch men" (5:10). And so the Master encouraged the crestfallen disciple by expressing confidence in his future. Jesus was now repeating the call to discipleship, but this time it was an affirmation, not an invitation: "From now on you *will* catch men." Jesus knew that finally the time had come when his men were ready to drop *everything* and follow him—and they did.

Admiral William "Bull" Halsey, who commanded the American naval fleet during World War II, said, "There are no great men in this world—only ordinary men who rise to meet great challenges." These common fishermen became great in this moment, for they answered life's most important challenge.

It is a leadership art-form to be able to salvage the dropout. Rescuing the discouraged, the frightened, the one who has slipped back into debilitating sin, must be mastered. Otherwise, too many good men and women fall between the cracks. Jesus teaches us, through the progressive method of developing laborers, that the dropout syndrome can be reduced significantly by slowly bringing our would-be disciples to total commitment *in stages.*

First, in the case of the early disciples, he provided a four-month introductory course in ministry ("Come and see"), followed by a short but meaningful opportunity to think it over. Only then did he directly challenge them ("Come and follow me").

It was after Jesus allowed his disciples to return to fishing that they began to have second thoughts. Jesus did not expect total commitment yet; this would come later in the third phase of training ("Come and be with me").

A shrewd salesman learns early that if prospective buyers have an opportunity to go away and mull things over with family and friends, the percentage of sales decreases. But in the case of the disciples, this episode by the Sea of Galilee was necessary to further cement their conviction. This solidifying of commitment took place when they realized the sufficiency of the Master to meet their needs.

After the miracle of the fish, the men were ready to go out with Jesus one more time, more committed than ever. They were now prepared because their call to discipleship had been confirmed. Jesus had handled his disciples with love, patience, and reassurance. There was no hint of sarcasm, browbeating, or degrading in his handling of these men. He did not get angry or give ultimatums. He chose to teach rather than denounce.

The disciples knew now that their failure didn't affect their Master's love for them or dilute his confidence in their potential. They were beginning to trust Jesus because they recognized that he cared for them.

'I am willing!'

We live in a world that is often cruel. It is easy to think that no one cares. There was a man who approached Jesus one day with this kind of perspective—he truly thought no one cared about him. The man had good reason to reach this conclusion, for he was a victim of leprosy. He knew that his affliction was terminal. There was pain in his joints, his skin had become thick and ugly, he had lesions on his face, and a foul discharge flowed from his sores. His entire body was wasting away.

According to the Jewish law, a leper had to wear torn clothes and allow his hair to hang loose. When approaching others, he was to cover his upper lip and scream, "Unclean! Unclean!" If he desired to attend synagogue, he had to peek through a squint hole. The leper was the lowest of society, despised by all.

But there was within this man something deep inside that kept hope alive that someday things would get better. He had heard of a great healer; news of this miracle worker had spread like a wind-blown grass fire. The leper couldn't help but ask the question, "I wonder if he would help me? But, no. I could never get close to him. He would run like the rest. I'm unclean. He would surely heed the law."

Nevertheless, if a man is truly desperate he won't let a few unanswered questions stop him. And so the unclean leper followed behind the crowd as the people pressed against Jesus. He calculated the right time, and when it came, he flung himself into the open screaming, "Unclean! Unclean!" The people immediately dispersed around him. Then, falling on his knees before Jesus, and with all the feeling and faith he could muster, he made a wonderful statement: "If you are willing, you can make me clean" (Mark 1:40). He didn't say, "If you can," but, "If you are willing." This poor man, who had been humbled beyond understanding by the wrath of his disease and his fellow-man, was rich enough in discernment to recognize Jesus' ability to heal.

At this point, the Healer of healers approached the trembling man. "Filled with compassion, Jesus reached out his hand and touched the man. 'I am willing,' he said. 'Be clean'" (Mark 1:41). The literal rendering for "filled with compassion" is "to open up the insides." Scripture teaches us that if we see a need and have the means to meet that need, and yet we close up our hearts, then we don't have the love of God in us (1 John 3:17). Jesus said he was willing, and then he did the unheard of: he touched the untouchable. This was not guarded compassion, as in the case of the man who saw freezing, wet hitchhikers shivering alongside the road: he passed them by, but then he felt a twinge of guilt, or perhaps it was a mild form of compassion, and so he backed up his car and threw his gloves out the window. No, Jesus went *all the way*. He reached down and touched this diseased man with the greatest care God has to offer.

In touching the leper Jesus was violating the traditional Jewish custom. However, he directed the man to show himself to the priest, honoring the levitical code. But the ex-leper was so filled with the wonderment of one touched by the God of the universe, so exhilarated to be cleansed of his plague, that he failed to keep silence as the Healer had commanded.

Jesus teaches us how to care through his loving touch. Sin, like any sore, needs to be exposed. But we don't need to do it with a broad axe. Usually just a pin-prick in the right place does the trick. The lancing of deep-seated problems can be done in a kind and loving way. Jesus cared. "I am willing" are the sweetest words that any human can hear from the lips of God. Jesus wept over Jerusalem, was crushed by Lazarus' death, and I believe there were tears in his eyes as he spoke to the leper.

The difference between ministry and activity is concern. Mere activity wears us out; ministry builds us up. When warmth is felt, the message is heard. *Compassion is the motivational basis of meaningful ministry.* The difficulty of ministry, the carnality of Christians, and the corruption of human nature will smash any good vision. Therefore, when pressed to the wall, it is vitally important for the disciple to *care* enough to keep on going.

The men who followed Jesus were beginning to see clearly the effectiveness of caring. The news of the Healer was spreading so fast that he couldn't walk the streets without being swamped by hundreds. Jesus had to travel the back roads in order to avoid large crowds. He had to stay outside the towns "in lonely places" (Mark 1:45).

The disciples could have explained the ministry of Jesus in one word: *compassion.* If you truly care about people, they will beat a path to your door. I am not saying that you will become famous and need bodyguards or secret travel plans. But meeting needs never goes out of style. The foundation of ministry is caring, and the vital link to a caring spirit is a close communion with our heavenly Father

A faith that dares

We have seen how Jesus established in the disciples' minds the basics of effective ministry: the word of God and prayer. Jesus was breeding conviction in them concerning these first two fundamentals of discipleship.

Ironically, however, even if disciples are strongly grounded in Scripture and prayer, they could conceivably find themselves failing to please God. How could his happen? There is a fundamental quality essential in all the basics of ministry; without this quality the basics become academic and difficult. "Without *faith* it is impossible to please God" (Hebrews 11:6). Faith is defined in Hebrews 11:1 as "being

sure of what we hope for and certain of what we do not see."
The following account from Mark 2:1-12 spells out the kind
of faith that pleases God in a way everyone can understand.

We find ourselves in the city of Capernaum on the
northern coast of the Sea of Galilee. Beside the main road
that runs through town sits a line of square, box-shaped
houses built of stone. The roofs are made of saplings inter-
twined with sand, mud, and a tar-like substance. Tiles over-
lay this earthy mixture, making the roofs two-feet thick. One
particular house catches our attention because of the crowds
of people swelling around it. In the center of the tightly
packed house is Jesus. His fame as the miraculous Healer
has spread like wildfire, and the sick follow him incessantly.
The people will not be put off. They want to touch him—to
have him touch them.

Jesus is preaching, and as we look at the crowd we are
amazed at the mix: the critical scribes, the grateful disciples,
and the needy, all of them hanging on every word, all for
different reasons. Suddenly, Jesus' message is punctuated by
a loud pounding on the roof. First there is a crack, then a
pole being pushed down to the floor, followed by a shower
of shingles and dirt. The faces of men appear, and they
lower something wrapped in a carpet. As the pallet reaches
eye-level, everyone gasps, for there is a man in it. The man
lies paralyzed, unable to even reach out for help.

Now all eyes turn to Jesus for his reaction. Some are
upset that such a wonderful message is interrupted. But Jesus
is an opportunist, and class is always in session. He kneels
down, looks up at the roof, and a smile plays across his face.
He is pleased, and so he says to the paralytic, "Son, your sins
are forgiven" (Mark 2:5). The people marvel at this statement, exchanging quick glances. Some faces show amazement, and some show joy. The faces of the scribes, though,
are filled with rage. They quickly confer among themselves,

and then they proclaim the entire incident blasphemous. Now the ball is in Jesus' court again. He explains his statement, and then he tells the man to take up his bed and walk. And he does! A crippled man is healed!

The quality demonstrated in this incident that particularly pleased Jesus was *faith*. He desired that all those present clearly understand that this crippled man was pleasing to him. Without the key ingredient of faith, this scene would never have happened. One characteristic of true faith is that it creates situations that give God glory and meet the needs of his people.

By retracing our steps through this story, we can glean the characteristics of a faith that pleases God.

> Some men came, bringing to him a paralytic, carried by four of them. Since they could not get him to Jesus because of the crowd, they made an opening in the roof above Jesus and, after digging through it, lowered the mat the paralyzed man was lying on. (Mark 2:3-4)

These men dared to move against the odds. The first characteristic of a faith that pleases God is *daring to face the difficult*. They had to carry the body through the crowd in the face of the complaints of others closer to the house who didn't want to give up their place. In addition, there was the hoisting of the body onto the roof itself against the probable protests of the owner. They demonstrated great belief in the person of Jesus by acting in spite of tradition and decorum

G. K. Chesterton wrote, "Christianity has not been tried and found wanting; it has been found difficult and not tried." The Christian must not allow difficulty to stop him. Great Britain, during World War II, found itself in perilous, seemingly hopeless times. But a short, pudgy man named Winston Churchill stood before the radio microphone and inflated the sagging spirits of the British people with the power of his words.

Why was Churchill able to inspire the hearts of frightened people in the darkest of hours? The answer: *faith.* The people caught a vision of faith in the rightness of the British cause. Faith is able to see the facts with the hope of things being changed. Churchill could see the end result of an Allied victory; he could see what his discouraged nation at first could not.

Faith often flies in the face of logic and the facts as we see them. What we are often challenged to believe seems laughable from our limited perspective. Mary was confronted by an angel telling her that she was with child, even though she knew she was a virgin. But she trusted in God despite the apparent contradiction.

Another feature of faith is that *it dares to be different.* It is not easy to stand out in a crowd as different from everyone else. The innovator who risks coloring outside the lines of tradition, as did Jesus himself, will be open for criticism and discouragement. These men who came through the roof could have looked for healing in another, more conventional way. For example, they could have presented the paralytic man's need to a priest through the sacrificial system. But they were willing to take an unorthodox approach, which seemed to please Jesus, for he perceived their faith (2:5). There was no rebuke from the Master for breaking up the meeting. He was always willing to be interrupted by faith.

Throughout this experience the disciples were learning about what kind of faith pleases God. Everything we do teaches. Good or bad, we are teaching all the time. Thus we must be more aware of the many sermons we are preaching without even knowing it. More than what Jesus *said* about faith, it is what he *did* in response to faith that left its mark in the final analysis.

When the Jewish teachers sarcastically asked, "Who can forgive sins but God alone?" (2:7), they were right in a sense, for Scripture teaches that only God can release man from his sinful plight. But there was something irreverent and faithless in their attitude. Jesus countered their indignant question with another question: "Which is easier: to say to the paralytic, 'Your sins are forgiven,' or to say, 'Get up, take your mat and walk'?" (2:9).

Any religious charlatan could say to a man, "Your sins are forgiven." However, very few men have ever said to a cripple, "Take up your bed and walk," with positive results. For man, the two statements are very different. The first has no credibility without the second. To God, the first is no more difficult than the second. But to man, the first is the most important. Sin was the core issue, and the forgiveness of sin, the main mission of the Savior. Jesus condescended to their level for the purpose of making an important point. He would heal the man so that they would know that he had the power to forgive sins (2:8-12). It was through the same power that he performed the healing. As the man exited through the crowd, all were amazed, including the Jewish teachers.

The attitude of these legalistic Jews parallels a certain segment of the Christian community that needs to be understood and changed. There is a subtle but tenacious rebellion of unbelief thwarting the purposes of God from within the Church. True disciples need to stand up to such a legalistic undercurrent when it occurs. Jesus himself exposed the hardness and unbelief of the legalists, thus stirring up the spirit of envy residing in them. Jesus was a threat to a way of life they held dear.

One of the most permanent things in life is change. The harder the heart, the more closed the mind—closed, legalistic, and ugly. The scribal attitude within the Church today must be understood, resisted, and purged.

Faith that pleases God is a faith that won't quit. It dares to face the difficult, it is willing to be different, and it goes over, under, around, and through difficulties. Faith brings about new and creative methodology, which is almost inevitably opposed by the scribal attitude.

Another aspect of faith that pleases God is that *the results are dynamic.* The people who observed the healing of the paralytic were all "amazed" (2:12). The Greek word for *amazed* also means "in ecstasy." The crowd was thrilled with the results. They even praised God!

This experience encouraged the disciples to develop a faith that pleased God. The old saying goes, "Behold the turtle: he makes progress only when he sticks out his neck." How many people are willing to take a chance, to dare to be different, to take on the opposition? The results are certainly worth it, for they come from a God who is pleased. And why is he pleased? Because faith creates amazement in the human mind and spirit, causing man to give glory to God.

True disciplemaking is difficult because it entails change, it takes a long time, and it is hard to visualize. It is teeming with both possibilities and problems. As in the case of the disciples, who had to launch out into deep water to confirm their call, each person who decides to follow the Master must launch out in faith, taking chances and facing the challenges of building other disciples. I once read an inscription on the side of a building: "A man who sees the invisible, hears the inaudible, believes the incredible, and thinks the unthinkable." This kind of person is a disciple.

6
BOTH FEET IN THE
REAL WORLD

In the spiritual realm there are two primary ways to grow. The first is through trouble and trials (Romans 5:3-4, James 1:2-4). But how many of us want to sit around and wait for trouble before we can grow? Oh, it will come, but depending on trouble for growth is definitely a negative approach. The other option is stepping out in faith and experiencing the positive aspects of ministry. This second method is the one Jesus modeled for his men.

The cause of every problem is change. My wife and I had always considered ourselves very calm-natured people. It was hard to identify with those people who lost their tempers, particularly those who let their children drive them to fits of anger and frustration. When I saw our first son through the nursery window, I couldn't wait to get that little bundle of joy home so I could start meeting his needs.

Three and a half days later I learned some surprising things about human nature—mostly mine, unfortunately. I found out I didn't like taking care of babies. My son had no regard for my needs. He didn't care that I required a good night's sleep in order to get up fresh in the morning. He would scream and scream, until I finally had to nudge my wife to get up and take care of him. There were times when I was inclined to take that little bundle of joy and spank his sweet little back-side. It was amazing what a little change could do to create havoc in our lives, revealing to our chagrin the darker side of our nature.

Growth presupposes change. In fact, for a growing person there is nothing as permanent as change. But all this changing creates problems: new ways must be found as old ways fail, new habits formed as old ones are broken, new attitudes adopted as old ones die. Look behind any problem in your life and you will find a change of some sort. There are many people who want to be somebody, but who resist growth because growth requires change, and change is risky.

The nature of change can be seen in the way Jesus challenged the religious establishment. Although Jesus generally reached out in a positive manner, yet at the same time he created tension between himself and the spiritual leaders of Israel. Jesus' example seems to indicate that reaching out and encountering trouble is better than sitting around and waiting for it.

A doctor who made house calls

Jesus used an interesting metaphor to describe his effect on the religious establishment of his day: "No one pours new wine into old wineskins. If he does, the wine will burst the skins, and both the wine and the wineskins will be ruined. No, he pours new wine into new wineskins" (Mark 2:22).

Old wineskins are dry and brittle; they don't adapt well

to new wine. New wine causes the old bag to stretch, crack, and leak. The legalistic Jewish religious establishment, of course, was the old wineskin, and the new wine represented the teachings of Jesus. The Pharisees were suffering from hardening of the spiritual arteries. They were alarmed that Jesus invited Levi, a corrupt tax collector, to follow him. They were astonished that he touched and healed a social outcast, and aghast that he didn't practice the hyper-legalities of the Sabbath. There wasn't a Pharisee within miles who wouldn't have given his last denarius to get rid of this threat to their brittle religious system.

The name of the vital Christian life is *change*. The word *sanctification* implies that disciples should be changing, constantly becoming more like Christ (Romans 8:29, 2 Corinthians 3:18). The transformation of an ugly, hostile spirit at war with God into a loving spirit of beauty, is the goal of the Christian life. But transformation requires an inner change. The new wine of Christ places incredible pressure on a person's emotional, cultural, and spiritual life. Nevertheless, we have to be ready and willing to modify our wineskins. Jesus kept pouring out the new wine, thus creating an intense battle between himself and the religious establishment.

His first conflict with the Jewish legalists arose in the tense social setting subsequent to the calling of Levi, the tax collector.

> Once again Jesus went out beside the lake. A large crowd came to him, and he began to teach them. As he walked along, he saw Levi son of Alphaeus sitting at the tax collector's booth. "Follow me," Jesus told him, and Levi got up and followed him. (Mark 2:13-14)

Capernaum was a main thoroughfare joining major cities around the Sea of Galilee. Customs officials or tax collectors were stationed at most bridges and canals, and so Capernaum was a focus of taxation activity. Tax collectors were despised men. They took no salary; instead they received a commission based on their effectiveness in collecting taxes. The collectors, Levi among them, were commonly extortionists. Hatred for these men was so strong among the Jewish leaders that Jewish tax collectors were listed along with outcasts, murderers, and robbers. They were disqualified as judges and witnesses, and were excommunicated from the synagogue. Their families considered them either dead or a disgrace.

Jesus couldn't have chosen a more controversial figure for a spiritual encounter. One might get the idea that Jesus' selection of such an outcast was intentional. The Master was, after all, accustomed to doing shocking, unexpected things in order to make an important point, as when he cleared the temple or when he asked fishermen to launch out into the deep. To add insult to injury, Jesus changed Levi's name to Matthew. Name changes can be cosmetic: Marion Morrison to John Wayne, or Archie Leach to Cary Grant. But they can also be life-changing: Simon to Peter, meaning "Rock," and now the vile tax collector Levi to Matthew, meaning "Gift of God."

Jesus called Levi just as he called the others: "Follow me." And like the earlier disciples, Levi responded immediately. He followed because he had heard of Jesus; he knew there was something special about him. Also, Levi surely had an aching in his heart. Living as an outcast, despite one's material wealth, can be the most bitter experience in life. And so Levi followed Jesus because he offered him acceptance and hope to escape his plight.

According to Luke 5:29, Levi gave a big reception in his home. The man was thrilled. One day he was a despised degenerate, and the next day he was going into the ministry.

He threw himself a going away party so that he could introduce his friends to this extraordinary rabbi. But who would
come to an outcast's party? Other outcasts, of course. Mark
2:15 indicates that "sinners" were there. It is likely that there
were prostitutes, winos, wheeler-dealers, gamblers, extortionists, and other assorted riffraff there to see what Levi was
up to now.

Earlier Jesus had taught his disciples by example the
critical principle of reaching the world where it is ripest.
Jesus was grateful for the opportunity to talk with the immediate contacts from Levi's world. The average Christian
suffers from a tendency to lose all non-Christian friends
soon after conversion. The new Christian, however, still
knows scores of people who are naturally curious about their
friend's new-found faith. The fresh believer is usually anxious to share his new life of love and joy. Jesus teaches us to
tap this resource, making ourselves available to the friends
and relatives of the newly converted.

By communicating, via example, that this was a priority,
Jesus gave the disciples one of the keys that caused the early
Church to grow quite rapidly. The most effective way to
reach people is to utilize the natural networks of families,
fraternal organizations, neighborhoods, and common-ground
activities.

The most common problem of outreach in our discipleship groups is finding non-Christians to invite to activities. Unfortunately, many Christians drift apart from their
non-Christian friends. Even experienced Christians tend to
insulate themselves from meaningful contact with the outside world.

Jesus was enjoying himself at Levi's banquet. He loved
to talk with and minister to the hungry hearts of receptive
sinners. The reception probably had a positive, warm, open
atmosphere. Unfortunately, this was soon to change. Enter

the party-poopers, the custodians of the religious shell, the keepers of the inflexible wineskins of tradition. "When the teachers of the law who were Pharisees saw him eating with the 'sinners' and tax collectors, they asked his disciples: 'Why does he eat with tax collectors and "sinners"'?"

The scribes and the Pharisees were the orthodox religious leaders of the ecclesiastical establishment. Their stated purpose was to protect the integrity of the Law. They could not be faulted for this basically good intention, but, as C. S. Lewis said, "Heresy is the truth taken too far." The Pharisees had allowed their zeal for religious trivia to blind them to the spiritual truth, and so they turned their relatively good intentions against God himself.

To these "religious" men, Jesus' eating and drinking with the scum of society was an outrage. These sinners were the ritually "unclean" people of the land who didn't hold to the scribal traditions. Most orthodox Jews would have no contact with such scoundrels, not even to talk with them or to do business. By breaking with this precedent of the religious cold-shoulder, Jesus had offended these legalistic vigilantes. He had stretched their wineskin to the breaking point.

Jesus despised the theological types who majored in showing off their righteousness. By their legalism, the hypocritical Pharisees prevented honest seekers from approaching God. Caustic, critical, judgmental, suspicious, and unforgiving, they sought to control all the ministries of God. They faulted anyone outside of their ranks. Jesus acutely described their hypocrisy: "John came neither eating nor drinking, and they say, 'He has a demon.' The Son of Man came eating and drinking, and they say, 'Here is a glutton and a drunkard, a friend of tax collectors and 'sinners''' (Matthew 11:18-19). The legalists were not satisfied either way, and so they slandered both John and Jesus.

Jesus answered their criticism of his befriending

"sinners" with an ancient proverb, followed by a statement of purpose: "It is not the healthy who need a doctor, but the sick. I have not come to call the righteous, but sinners" (Mark 2:17). Sin is a spiritual sickness. But the patient will not want a doctor unless he knows he is sick. Although the self-righteous scribes thought (erroneously) that they were spiritually healthy, Levi and his friends freely admitted that they were spiritually sick. And Jesus was the kind of spiritual doctor who was willing to make house calls. He recognized the real world—a world of many great needs, the greatest being the need for salvation from sin.

The fatal mistake of the Pharisees is still common today among evangelical Christians. We have mistakenly identified the unbeliever as the enemy rather than the victim of the enemy.[1] We have erected unnecessary barriers between ourselves and the very ones we pray to reach. These barriers are usually cultural, not theological.

We often communicate a legalistic attitude that says, "If you practice certain activities, you are not welcome in the Christian community." Therefore, the non-believer receives an inflexible, judgmental attitude from the very ones who should be accepting him. The Christian community must keep the unbeliever's view of salvation uncluttered with cultural biases. We need to keep the message of salvation simple and pure, just as Jesus modeled it for us.

We can refuse to condone, without condemning, the non-Christian for practices that, though unseemly, will not keep him out of heaven. Jesus was not winking at sin just because he appealed to sinners He was not saying that it is okay to be a prostitute, gambler, drunkard, liar, thief, or cheat. Certainly he was not authorizing adultery and divorce just because he spent time with the woman at the well.

The primary issue in Jesus' mind was that this motley crew of sinners needed help. Compassion for the needy was the driving force behind his ministry. Christians, like Jesus, must look upon the lost as the victim, those upon whom compassion is the most productive endowment. There is no impact without contact. Unless we go where the fish are, we won't catch any. The Pharisees weren't catching anyone; they were fishing in a stained-glass aquarium and were coming up empty. The reason the Church has been so inept in evangelism is partly due to the pharisaic unwillingness to live in *the real world.*

Jesus demonstrated that fishing for men means going where they are. If people feel accepted, then they will relax and open up, which would be very unlikely if a judgmental attitude were communicated to them. Some of the most open people, whose hungry hearts are ripe for the gospel, smoke, curse, and tell off-color jokes. The Christian who desires to reach them must be willing to encounter some corruption and adversity. I do not advocate participation in such unholy activity, nor do I promote total isolation from it. The more moderate track of a critical presence is advised. A mature Christian can survive in such an atmosphere on a limited basis and still not practice or condone any of the above questionable activities. The important thing is not to allow non-salvation issues to stand in the way of a person's eternal destiny.

Several years ago I played on a city league basketball team. The team reached the play-offs and we had to travel over the weekend to Dallas to play in the state tournament. The players knew of my faith in Christ, but had not questioned me.

Subsequent to that weekend, they confessed that they had dreaded going on the trip. They were sure that I would require that we all sing hymns, read Scriptures, and pray all the way to Dallas. What actually happened was, as we loaded the van for our trip, I assured them that they should behave as they normally would, which put them at ease. I wanted them to know that they were not under judgment, that I accepted them. Two hours later, eight grown men were crowded into the corner of the van, where I sat answering their questions concerning Christ. I consider the trip one of the most productive witnessing experiences of my life.

How many more episodes like this one could be ours if only we would look to Jesus as our model. I didn't participate in the questionable activities of some players that weekend. At the same time, neither did I condemn them for acting like non-Christians. Admittedly, one must be assured and strong in the face of this type of temptation. One must know his or her weaknesses. This type of ministry is not advised for the teenager who has not matured enough to influence his peer group. In order to be effective, the disciple must be able to influence the group, rather than to be influenced by it.

Jesus was mature. He possessed convictions and the courage to back them up. The disciple should get wise counsel prior to embarking on outreach of this type to help him determine whether he can stand constant exposure to a non-Christian environment. It would be misleading to imply that we need considerable counseling before we can witness adequately. We do, however, need other believers to confirm the fact that we are ready to stand alone.

It is simply not God's will that Christians become "rabbit-hole believers," just sticking our heads out for a peek at that nasty world every now and then. God requires more than insulation from those we are commanded to reach. Some believers rejoice that all their neighbors are Christians. Personally, I would be disappointed if this were my case. It is not unusual to hear someone "praise the Lord" for giving him all Christians to work with. Jesus, on the other hand, advised us to seek out places to live, work, and play where we have a lot of contact with unbelievers.

I am acquainted with a fine couple who have a deep desire to reach their friends with the gospel. These friends, however, are of the country club set—drinking, dancing, bridge, and extraordinary cuisine are the common denominators. This harvest field is certainly well-heeled, but just as destitute spiritually as any. This couple sought to reach their friends without participating in some of the above activities. This opened several key witnessing opportunities. Unfortunately, an older brother in the Lord learned of this upper-crust evangelism, and subsequently informed this caring couple that they were out of line and that God would not bless their efforts.

When consulted as to a proper course of action—knowing both the caring couple who was penetrating the country club for Christ and the well-meaning churchman who wasn't—I related a story. D. L. Moody was confronted by a critical brother who questioned his style of pulpit evangelism. Moody's response was, "How many people have you led to Christ lately?" The critical brother lowered his head, obviously embarrassed. Moody then said, "I like my method better than yours."

Disciples would be well advised to take a chapter from the life of Jesus, who ministered with both feet in the world. As Jesus himself said to the Father on our behalf, "My prayer is not that you take them out of the world but that you protect them from the evil one" (John 17:15). The disciple must be taught by both example and explanation how to reach the lost where they live, work, and play—in the real world. This is radical, and yet not overly radical; it is simply following the example of our Lord.

Dealing with the legalists

A perpetual conflict between Jesus and the keepers of the old wine bags was the issue of *tradition*. Usually tradition in and of itself is more positive than negative. For example, our family has decided to establish certain traditions that we desire to be carried on by our children. Every Christmas Eve we like to eat a certain type of meal, visit with the same friends, read the Christmas story, attend church, and then return home to open gifts. This type of tradition can be treasured and can help hold a family together. Nevertheless, oftentimes traditions can hinder God's will in our lives. The following account is such a time.

> Now John's disciples and the Pharisees were fasting. Some people came and asked Jesus, "How is it that John's disciples and the disciples of the Pharisees are fasting, but yours are not?"
>
> Jesus answered, "How can the guests of the bridegroom fast while he is with them? They cannot, so long as they have him with them. But the time will come when the bridegroom will be taken from them, and on that day they will fast." (Mark 2:18-20)

The subject was fasting, and the Pharisee's question was, "Why don't you fast, Jesus?" Fasting was required by law only one day a year: the Day of Atonement. During four of the other Jewish holidays, fasting was recommended. But none of these events was taking place in this instance. However, it had been established by the Pharisees, as a tradition, that Mondays and Thursdays were days of fasting. Thursday was also market day, and so the sanctimonious Pharisees would walk down the main thoroughfare, shouting to get attention. They would cover themselves with white ashes just to make sure everyone knew how spiritual they were. Jesus, of course, was totally disinterested in this charade, and didn't follow suit.

Jesus answered the inquiry about fasting by asking a

question about another kind of "tradition"—the Jewish wedding celebration (2:19). Essentially he asked, "You haven't been to a wedding reception where food was nonexistent, have you?" The answer was obviously *no*, and, as a matter of fact, marriage celebrations were of such a special nature in Israel that most wedding parties would last a week. Certain laws were suspended, people were allowed to miss work, and for many this was a very rare respite from bone-crushing work. A man would be crazy to fast during such a festive time. The bride and groom would never be forgiven for not providing a feast to be remembered.

Jesus' answer was not only a common, easy-to-understand metaphor, but it was weighted with meaning. He likened himself to the bridegroom and the disciples to the attendants, family, or friends. His message was, "I am here! The Messiah! This is a time for rejoicing, not mourning. They can fast all they want after I'm gone!"

Jesus' heart was not set aflame by the tedious traditions of the religious establishment. The Pharisees, however, were caged in ritual and tradition. They not only desired to keep the 613 legitimate commandments given in the Law, but the entire body of oral tradition as well.

The Pharisees' appetite for tradition stemmed from their obsession with controlling the religious activity of Israel. The threatened person is one who enjoys safeguards, who needs controls to limit variety. The Pharisaic tendency to weight the Jewish people with policy created a massive machinery that served as a major contributor to their stumbling over Jesus. Their traditions were protections from the new, the fresh, the creative, and, tragically, from the truth. The Church often labors under much the same weighty machinery, thus causing it to miss new and effective means of fulfilling its mission.

A real challenge in disciplemaking is the extracting of

people from the yoke of traditions that hinder their spiritual lives. Men and women who are established in the four basics or foundations of the Christian life (Scripture, prayer, fellowship, and witnessing) will experience a trust in the sovereignty of God. This trust leads to personal security, thus reducing the compulsion to control or limit what God is doing. A secure person enjoys the creative spirit of God and looks forward to the next invasion of the supernatural into the mundane.

Jesus did not bow down to counter-productive traditions. He spoke out against them as superfluous stumbling blocks that create more trouble than they are worth. The modern-day disciplemaker can do the same. We need to be enthusiastic about the *right* things. Everything we do teaches. The impression we leave will be made more by practice than by preaching.

People who start with hearts aflame rise quickly to leadership in the local church. After a steady dose of administrative headaches, however, the flame often dies out, the heart grows cold. Churches are sometimes organized to administer in-house maintenance at the expense of helping people grow. The duties of necessary church administration should be shared and rotated so that all leaders have the refreshing opportunity periodically to engage in person-to-person ministry. The gifted administrator should be no less established in Scripture, prayer, fellowship, and witnessing than the gifted teacher.

When a disciple deals only with buildings and grounds, he begins to believe that the most important aspect of church life is well-kept facilities or consistent cash flow. Conversely, when a disciple deals only with prayer, Bible study, and witnessing, he begins to consider administrative work boring and unspiritual. The proper placing of spiritual gifts is vital to success in the long haul, but variety of experience and appreciation of others' abilities will make for a well-rounded disciple. Furthermore, if administrative personnel are given a ministry sabbatical periodically, they will keep their spiritual life fresh.

Jesus was constantly being confronted by the religious legalists of his day. Legalism is the measuring of spirituality by external behavior. Mark 2:23-3:6 records a classic confrontation over technical obedience to the Law. Parallel accounts are found in Matthew 12:1-21 and Luke 6:1-11. The plot was now thickening as the Jews conspired to kill Jesus.

Jesus taught men to minister with both feet in the world. The best way to reach the needy is to be with them. Without contact, there can be no impact. The Master encountered, as most of his followers will, opposition in traditional religious quarters. Disciples on the front lines for Jesus sometimes get jabbed in the back. Learning to deal with such criticism for being effective in outreach is vital to survival in the harvest field. This was the very problem Jesus faced.

In evangelism, coping with resistance both from without and from within comes with the territory. Jesus aggravated the Pharisees simply by being himself.

> One Sabbath Jesus was going through the grainfields, and as his disciples walked along, they began to pick some heads of grain. The Pharisees said to him, "Look, why are they doing what is unlawful on the Sabbath?"
>
> He answered, "Have you never read what David did when he and his companions were hungry and in need? In the days of Abiathar the high priest, he entered the house of God and ate the consecrated bread, which is lawful only for priests to eat. And he also gave some to his companions."
>
> Then he said to them, "The Sabbath was made for man, not man for the Sabbath. So the Son of Man is Lord even of the Sabbath." (Mark 2:23-28)

On any other day, picking grain would have been per-mitted. On the Sabbath, however, there were thirty-nine categories of work strictly prohibited. Picking grain was one of them. Jesus was aware of this legalistic observance and knew that defying it would create yet another conflict. But the higher reality of his mission beckoned him onward.

The only reason the Pharisees raised their question was to jump Jesus on the sly, to trip him up on a technicality of the oral law, thus discrediting him. There was already a plan afoot to rid the land of this itinerant rabbi who dared to challenge centuries of legalistic tradition (Mark 3:6, John 5:18). The Pharisees considered Jesus to be a maverick, an iconoclast, a blasphemer. They attacked him with vehe-mence in every confrontation. Jesus answered their accusa-tions regarding the Sabbath by referring back to the exam-ple of David eating the sacred bread in the temple because he was hungry (Mark 2:25-27). When King David ate this bread that was to be consumed only by priests, he demon-strated the principle that hunger takes priority over ritual.

The meaning Jesus desired to convey to his disciples, via the vehicle of conflict, was that human need takes prece-dence over human law. The Sabbath was designed to give man enjoyment, not to enslave his spirit through a list of oppressive rules. Rules are simply an orderly way of meeting needs. The rules of the Pharisees, however, were subtle manmade means of oppressing people, creating guilty, frus-trated, unhappy legalists.

The Pharisees misunderstood God's original intention for the Sabbath. It was instituted for the benefit of man, to give him rest from his labor so that he could renew his body, mind, and spirit. It is ludicrous to believe that exercising the body on the Sabbath violates the biblical idea of rest. A change of pace or a bit of variety adds vitality to life, making the actual laboring more productive and tolerable.

The Sabbath principle is carried into the twentieth century in the context of Sunday. The principle of rest from labor is applied to the Lord's day. It is to be a day of celebration, enjoyment, and renewal.

My childhood was spent in a legalistic religious atmosphere where many activities were forbidden on Sunday. I grew to despise Sunday because that was the day I couldn't run and play. The emphasis seemed to be on prohibition. What a negative approach to the *Lord's* day. Imagine, setting aside a day for God in which the paramount concern is what we can't do! Can I spend money, should Grandma cook a large meal, can we work up a sweat or eat an egg that a hen laid on Sunday? Such an attitude is absurd.

What was Jesus' response to all this legalism? Shortly after the grain-picking incident he entered the synagogue, a holy place, on the Sabbath, a holy day (Mark 3:1). He then proceeded, in sight of all, to heal a man with a withered hand. Then, with a stern look and a sense of challenge, he asked, "Which is lawful on the Sabbath: to do good or to do evil, to save life or to kill?" (verse 4). The awestruck observers kept silent because, once again, Jesus had stumped them. They were dumbfounded. Many times the Gospels record that Jesus' statements were so profoundly true and liberating that the greatest theological minds of the day were stupefied.

As Jesus looked around at their guilty faces, his anger grew. He was truly grieved within because of the hardness of their hearts. Leaders often feel anger. Jesus was indeed infuriated several times. He was livid in particular with the Pharisees because of their spiritual callousness and hypocrisy (Matthew 23). It taxed his patience to observe their critical, inflexible attitudes, for they were erecting barriers that stood in the way of reaching the needy. It was an ugly stench in his nostrils.

As he told the man to stretch out his hand, Jesus seemed

to be saying indirectly to the Pharisees, "I will move toward human need regardless of your obsession with tradition and your misunderstanding of God's law." And, in the process, Jesus was determined to teach his men the priority of meeting needs. Whatever it takes to reach people with the gospel of mercy, a disciple should do it!

But the Church of Jesus Christ is laden with excess baggage, hindering it from effective outreach. We are much like a group of sun worshipers trekking off to the beach on a warm, sunny day, dressed in raincoats and rubber knee boots, with umbrellas in hand. We are equipped, all right, but not to reach the world, not to fulfill the Great Commission.

We must unload the heavy baggage that hinders us— the weight of social convention, the drag of traditional religious trappings, and the legalistic tendency to categorize spirituality, thus causing it to be cold, hard, and cruel. The world will sit up and take notice when the beauty of Jesus is seen in his Church. But the beauty that turns the world toward Christ at the same time threatens the pharisaic ones. The Pharisees immediately went out of that synagogue to plot how best to kill Jesus. We would do well to take the advice Jesus gave to the legalistic Pharisees: "Go and learn what this means: 'I desire mercy, not sacrifice'" (Matthew 9:13).

Jesus ministered with both feet in the world. He launched out into his world without being overly concerned about getting soiled. We, too, need to be willing to risk criticism from others in order to reach those in need. Such a commitment usually involves social interaction with those who practice different ethics. But as followers of the One who did not compromise, we are called to reach out to the people who are in need, breaking down the barriers by spending our time with them. This may entail going out to dinner with non-Christian neighbors rather than heading off to the Sunday school class party. People who are more concerned with their religious reputation than with the welfare of others will not understand. For they have chosen sacrifice over mercy.

If this perspective sounds radical, that's because it is! The reason it is radical rather than typical is that, in evangelism, the Church has often followed more in the steps of the Pharisees than in the steps of Jesus. What Jesus modeled *for* us should be commonplace *among* us, taking place every day all over the world. The way to take on *his* attitude is to start building bridges to the people in need. Some of the needs are physical, others are spiritual. We have been called to a rescue operation of *mercy*. Evangelism itself is a merciful way of trying to meet a spiritual need. Witnessing should never be contrived; rather it should flow naturally out of everyday life. God has provided us with contacts galore in the marketplace, community, and even in some religious settings. And he has revealed the fact that the secret to reaching the needy is simply keeping spiritually alert to all the hungry hearts around us.

The "Come and follow me" stage of ministry-training was a time when Jesus established his men in three of the four basics of discipleship. In the synagogue he established the priority of using *the word of God* in ministry (Mark 1:21-28). Then he demonstrated the priority of *prayer* when he left the crowds behind to go talk with his Father (Mark 1:35-38). The nature of *witnessing* was modeled by our Lord amid great controversy with the legalistic Pharisees (Mark 2:15-17). After a disciple is established in these basics, then he needs to flex his wings by reaching out to others. Effective outreach means going out into the *real* world where the needy are, rather than pursuing the spiritually artificial world inhabited by the legalistic Pharisees. As all the followers of Jesus Christ go through this "Come and follow me" phase of ministry, they gradually go through that critical transition from sincere converts to established disciples.

Footnotes:
1. Joseph Aldrich, *Life-Style Evangelism* (Portland: Multnomah Press, 1981).

7
OUR SPIRITUAL BONDING FORCE

There is a chasm that often exists between us in our personal relationships. Sometimes it seems impossible to build a bridge across that chasm . . . but it isn't. People desperately need to be brought together in true fellowship. But how can that be accomplished? How can the family of God be truly united as a family should be? What bridge can adequately span across that chasm?

There are many different ideas about the true nature of fellowship. Some people consider fellowship to be coffee and doughnuts, along with discussions about the world, the weather, and work. Others see it as a well-oiled machine designed by God to massage and lubricate people right into the Church. But what is the true biblical perspective on fellowship?

The Greek word for fellowship, *koinonia,* means "something in common." What Christians have in common is an uncommonly sublime personal relationship with God through Jesus Christ. It is in the Messiah alone that we find our spiritual bonding force.

A holy foundation

As we look now to the life of Jesus to find the nature of true fellowship, we see him standing there in Jerusalem surrounded by some angry, legalistic Jews. As usual, they are upset about a breach of their Sabbath laws. There was nothing new in the charges they were bringing against Jesus, except that they were now so aggravated that the plot to kill him was intensifying rapidly (John 5:10-18). There remained at minimum a year and a half to the Cross.

It was in the tension-packed context of this growing pressure that Jesus zeroed in on the essence of fellowship. The Master responded to the vicious attacks of the Jews regarding his actions on the Sabbath by referring to his relationship with his Father. "Jesus said to them, 'My Father is always at his work to this very day, and I, too, am working'" (John 5:17). In this statement he was implying that his actions (in this case the healing of a paralytic man on the Sabbath) were directly related to his Father's way of doing good things, even on the Sabbath! But this statement incensed the Jews even more than the Sabbath issue, for it clearly implied Jesus' divine nature (5:18).

Jesus decided to give the Jews the full picture of the Father-Son relationship. He described that Family fellowship in terms of dependency, love, knowledge, power, and honor (5:19-30). We see in this passage that the most primary characteristic of fellowship with God is *submission*. Jesus was in such intimate spiritual communion with his Father that he would not do something until he first saw the Father doing it (5:19), thus demonstrating a truly humble attitude.

Although he appeared on the surface to be an eccentric Jewish rabbi, Jesus was in direct communication with heaven! He identified the Father God as the *source* of his ability to minister and the *authority base* of his actions. He summed up his divine fellowship with the Father in a remarkable statement: "By myself I can do nothing; I judge only as I hear, and my judgment is just, for I seek not to please myself but him who sent me" (5:30). Although he once resided with the Father in the glorious setting of the divine realm, he "did not consider equality with God something to be grasped, but made himself nothing, taking the very nature of a servant, being made in human likeness. And being found in appearance as a man, he humbled himself . . ." (Philippians 2:6-8). The Son humbled himself by submitting to his Father, living out his earthly existence as the God-man.

A crucial part of faith is submission—believing that God is who he claims to be, and coming humbly before him. If we come before God in humility, then we can submit to his will; we can understand that he alone is our source for ministry and our authority for everything we do and say. This intimate, foundational relationship with God was first modeled by Jesus. He perpetuated his close relationship with his Father through constant communication. The Gospels often mention that Jesus went off by himself to pray. All meaningful relationships are developed and maintained through regular communication. Jesus labored fervently in prayer to discern the Father's will.

Jesus could submit totally because he knew that the Father loved him totally (5:20). The Son submitted, even though to do so meant persecution. The key to the God-man's endurance in these difficult times of persecution was his fellowship with his Father. This close relationship provided him with the support, guidance, and power he needed.

Here is the way to vital, effective fellowship: *Our vertical relationship with God shapes our horizontal relationship with those around us.* Fellowship with God is even more fundamental than fellowship with men. Only when we develop a humility of spirit and a willingness to submit to God will we be able to develop an open, honest kind of sharing (*koinonia*), giving us strength, support, and guidance for our lives. This is the holy foundation on which we must build.

The spiritual cornerstone for all Christians is Christ himself. Our intimate fellowship with Christ prepares us for meaningful fellowship with Christians. Solid relationships with one another are possible only when they are built around the solid relationship we have with the Father through his Son. There is a direct correlation between these two distinct kinds of fellowship. The discipler whose walk with God is vibrant and meaningful will pass on his fervor to those around him. In this way, true fellowship tends to keep growing in quality and quantity.

Christians make a serious mistake when they seek their primary fellowship in their relationships with other Christians. Whenever we depend on other people for our spiritual vitality, we are deceiving ourselves, and in the long run we will find only frustration. Placing fellowship with others before fellowship with God creates weak, bewildered believers. Such self-limiting fellowship will tear us down, rather than build us up.

The individual Christian must develop his own walk with God. This is why personal devotions are so vital to effective Christian living. Jesus spent time with his Father in order to receive sustenance for his mission. The application, then, is for a disciple to establish communication with God on a regular basis as part of his lifestyle. Those who set aside time to communicate with God through prayer and Bible study can experience a relationship similar to the one Jesus had with his Father. What more could we want? Only those who are desperate search for something spectacular beyond what is already sublime. Dietrich Bonhoeffer incisively explained this folly:

> One who wants more than what Christ has established does not want Christian brotherhood. He is looking for some extraordinary social experience which he has not found elsewhere; he is bringing muddled and impure desires into Christian brotherhood. Just at this point Christian brother-hood is threatened most often at the very start by the greatest danger of all, the danger of being poisoned at its root, the danger of confusing Christian brotherhood with some wish-ful idea of religious fellowship, of confounding the natural desire of the devout heart for community with the spiritual reality of Christian brotherhood.[1]

Unless we are walking with God, we hinder true community and sabotage our own witness. If we are not in tune with him, our judgment will be clouded and our fellowship empty. Such superficial fellowship constitutes no more than socializing. The main topic of discussion is usually somewhat mundane. Thus people do not reveal who they really are, for they are afraid of not being accepted.

The reason the room usually becomes silent when the question is asked of Christians, "What has God been doing in your lives lately?" is because of the lack of true fellowship with God. If we are not consistently in the word and prayer, communicating with our Father, then our Christian walk will be frustrating and theoretical, primarily academic. But when Christians are enlivened by their relationship with God, then their fellowship is dynamic, and when the above question is asked, the leader has trouble quieting them down.

Jesus needed fellowship with his Father because he was on the front lines of ministry. The disciples needed fellowship with with Jesus and with one another because they were in the heat of the battle. Spirit-controlled believers who communicate with God and do his will *need* fellowship in order to be sustained in their daily lives.

Characteristics of fellowship

In order to understand the nature of true fellowship, we need to examine it organically. Then we will be able to build better bridges between ourselves and others. Here are four basic characteristics of fellowship:

1. *Effective fellowship is characterized by total acceptance.* Jesus knew that his Father loved him. In a context of acceptance a person feels free to share his joys and concerns without fear of rejection. We need the freedom to talk of our hurts as well as our joys. For several years I met monthly with a group of pastors in a setting of mutual trust and acceptance. We had nothing to prove to each other, nothing to hide. We shared our deepest struggles and hurts, and even now I treasure the therapeutic effect of that group. Just as Jesus was accepted by his Father and as he accepted his men, we too need a setting in which we can deal with our innermost needs together with our trustworthy comrades.

2. *Effective fellowship is based on a person's fellowship with God.* When a disciple spends regular time with God in prayer and in God's word, then and only then will he be able to share in the life of Christ. Silence is not golden when it comes to sharing with and encouraging others in the body. A disciple needs to share what God is teaching him—fresh insights from the word and answers to prayer. This kind of sharing will encourage others to develop a closer walk with God.

The thesis proposed earlier bears repeating: Solid fellowship with Christ leads to solid fellowship with Christians. The quality of our fellowship with others is directly linked to the quality of our fellowship with God. The key is communication, and the primary communication vehicles are God's word and prayer.

3. *Effective fellowship includes the basic dynamics of spiritual life.* These dynamics are detailed in the book of Acts, which describes the first years of the Church. The infant Church had many dynamic activities, which helps to explain its rapid growth and good health. "They devoted themselves to the apostles' teaching and to the fellowship, to the breaking of bread and to prayer. . . . All the believers were together . . ." (Acts 2:42-44). Being together is very natural and fundamental for the Church. In our culture, we have to work at togetherness, because our lives become so complex and diffused. Usually Christians of our culture do not have "everything in common" (Acts 2:44), whether material or spiritual things. But there *are* certain ways for us to develop vibrant fellowship:

Eating together (Acts 2:42)—"The love feast," a large meal shared by all believers once a week in the early Church, was followed by Communion. Nothing knocks down barriers quicker than eating a meal together. When we eat, we share in a common need, making it easy for us to relax and talk informally. Sharing in Communion around the Lord's table is an in-depth experience that can lead to lifelong friendships.

Praying together (Acts 2:42)—Praying together binds the hearts of disciples, creating a sense of mutual commitment. As we appeal to God in areas of need, we learn to really care about our brothers and sisters. As we pray together, we build faith and cement our relationships.

Singing together (Acts 2:47)—Praising God requires a release of the heart. The most noble act of any disciple is to worship and praise the Lord of the universe. A Spirit-filled person is one with a song in his heart for God (Ephesians 5:19). Disciples should, with one voice, praise the Lord for his greatness. There is a therapeutic nature to music, one that we should not neglect in our times of fellowship with God and with our brothers and sisters.

Playing together—Creative recreation is vital to positive relationships. My congregation needs to see me sometimes without a coat and tie. Sometimes we just need to laugh together. Sure, the Lord's work is serious business. But we need to periodically get together just to play in order to remind ourselves that we are human beings, more alike than we are different. A few potbellies, knock knees (mine), and varicose veins do wonders in breaking down barriers.

Eating together, praying together, singing together, and playing together will gradually knit disciples into a cohesive unit capable of accomplishing great things for God. This kind of fellowship produces a powerful outreach (Acts 2:45-47). The early disciples reached out open-heartedly to others. They sold or gave away most of what they had. Consequently, there were people added to their number on a daily basis. These generous disciples were positive, enthusiastic, and filled with a sense of wonder concerning all that God was doing. This type of witness to the world is possible only when all the necessary ingredients are present.

4. *Effective fellowship meets not only general needs, but also specific needs.* Each person needs someone close to him to minister to his specific needs. "As iron sharpens iron, so one man sharpens another" (Proverbs 27:17). The metaphor in this proverb is telling us that we need someone close to us who can help to knock off the rough edges of our character. Specific needs can be dealt with most effectively by a one-on-one kind of ministry. Some of the most important growth times in my life have been together with an older, more mature man, absorbing his wise counsel for my life.

Another reason for one-on-one ministry is found in Ecclesiastes:

> Two are better than one, because they have a good return for
> their work: If one falls down, his friend can help him up. But
> pity the man who falls and has no one to help him up! (Eccle-
> siastes 4:9-10)

Everyone needs someone to pick him up during difficult
times. There have been several people I have looked to for
encouragement. The listening ear and the sound advice
they have given has kept me in ministry. A pastor has special
needs not shared by most Christians. The same thing is true
of other professions and callings.

Proverbs 27:17 is saying, in effect, that we need a friend
to encourage us or perhaps to kick us in the seat of the pants
when we need it. As we proceed on our spiritual pilgrimage,
we need to give and receive the full orb of fellowship mentioned in 1 Thessalonians 5:14: "Warn those who are idle,
encourage the timid, help the weak, be patient with everyone."

We all need someone to interact with us in all these
ways. This is the type of ministry that cannot be adequately
handled in any other context, even in the small group. Every
disciple has personal needs that must be met in a one-to-one
way. Christian fellowship is really meaningful only when
there is an opening up of hearts. Only when we open up and
allow ourselves to be ministered to in an intimate way will we
learn how to minister to others. We need to learn how to
"spur one another on toward love and good deeds" (Hebrews
10:24). Every person has specific needs that must be targeted
by a trusted mentor who has taken the time and put forth the
effort to develop a meaningful one-to-one relationship.

If we take a good look at Jesus' disciples at this point in
our study, we notice that they were not really *laboring* in the
harvest field as much as they were *watching*. One immediate
application for the discipler is that he should not push the

labor of ministry on disciples too early. The longer the disciples watched Jesus, the more natural his style of ministry seemed to be, and the more secure they were in their understanding of what needed to be done.

Because of a long time of observation and limited participation (nearly a full year), the disciples were saved much time and many a headache later. If I had ten years to achieve a goal in some field in which I was unfamiliar, I would spend the first three learning from a successful model, then the remaining seven working on my assignment. We shouldn't be surprised that Jesus didn't initiate his multiplication of ministry until he was confident that the disciples understood the mechanics of ministry.

The disciples did not make the transition from a small group of converts being established in the basics to a ministry team composed of skilled spiritual laborers until the third phase of ministry training—"Come and be with me." When they did make this transition, it was natural because they were thoroughly schooled and established in the word of God, prayer, witnessing, and fellowship.

There can be no advancing without retreating
Retreating is an essential step in the spiritual growth process. This is not simply my casual conclusion; it was first taught and practiced by our Lord. Mark 3:7 states, "Jesus withdrew with his disciples to the lake." This was not the only occasion when Jesus withdrew from the needy crowd because of his own needs. He took his disciples off on retreat on a regular basis. They needed time alone for rest, relaxation, and recharging of their spiritual reserves. There is an axiom that describes the need for retreating: Come apart or you will come apart. Ministry life is not a sprint; it is a long-distance event.

Jesus wanted his men to know the value of pacing. A

person who counts the cost and plans the ministry course is much more likely to finish and accomplish great things than the irregular sprinter. We are not able to effectively advance in ministry without periodically retreating. William Carey told a friend, "Whatever you say of me, say that I was a plodder." The fresh, well-disciplined person with a balance to his life will, in the long run, be more productive for God. Therefore, the value of retreating should be learned early and practiced regularly, for it can be a valuable dimension in our development of vital fellowship.

Our relationships with God and with our fellow Christians should both be continually cultivated throughout the course of our lives. We will not become truly *established* in ministry until we place a priority on these two forms of fellowship. The primary vehicle for establishing disciples in ministry is the small group. And yet there are also those special, essential times alone with God or with one close friend who knows us very well. Man is a social creature: We must never lose sight of this fact.

Footnotes:
   1. Dietrich Bonhoeffer, *Life Together* (New York: Harper and Row, 1954), page 26.

PRINCIPLES AND SUGGESTIONS

1. *Call people who have prepared hearts.* Often leaders spend more time trying to motivate people who aren't interested than they spend with those who are already interested. But bestowing responsibility on the unfaithful, the disinterested, and the carnal is the zenith of folly. Be on the lookout for the hungry hearts— those who are champing at the bit to be established in the word of God, prayer, fellowship, and witnessing.

2. *Take the responsibility on yourself to train people.* Your disciples should know that they will not be asked to do anything for which they have not been trained. The responsibility to teach them, train them, and model for them is yours.

3. *Be sure to withhold threatening information.* It is quite

dangerous to overload disciples with information, even good information. Give them a little information at a time, show them how it works, then let them try it. After they have tried it, critique them so that they can refine it and try it again. But never rush them through this process.

4. *Call your disciples to a vision.* Along with their investment of time and energy, your disciples need to have a vision for their pursuit of ministry. Whenever someone begins recruiting people effectively to a vision, the Christian community sits up and takes notes.

5. *Establish your disciples in the four fundamentals of discipleship.* To "establish" the word of God, prayer, fellowship, and witnessing means to make them a habitual part of our lives. Without the establishing of disciples in these four fundamentals, there would be no disciples, because these disciplines form the spiritual life-support system for *all* Christians.

6. *Develop commitment in your disciples in stages.* The commitment of Jesus' twelve disciples increased progressively over a three-year period. You as a discipler need to intentionally plan a long-term process if you want your disciples to grow in their dedication and ministry skills.

7. *Establish a clear set of priorities.* Jesus combined schedule with compassion, planning with flexibility. The discipler must live in a way that communicates this same balance, setting goals and priorities, and then establishing a corresponding schedule. It will take *discipline* to keep that schedule but also *flexibility* to alter it when appropriate.

8. *Respond to both success and adversity with prayer.* When the crowds desired to crown Jesus king of Israel, pressured him to heal them, and surrounded him with their plots, he withdrew to pray. When your disciples see you react to both victory and crisis with prayer, they will become impressed with the priority of prayer.

9. *Handle "drop-outs" with care.* When his disciples returned to fishing after their first exposure to ministry, Jesus didn't denounce them or degrade them in any way. Rather, he reaffirmed his acceptance of them, emphasizing the potential they had for future ministry. When you see disciples begin to manifest a "drop-out" attitude of disillusionment and regular tardiness, draw them back with positive reinforcement, not with negative criticism.

10. *Show your disciples that faith pleases God.* Faith in the living God will help your disciples to grow immeasurably. Faith that pleases God cares to be different and is willing to stand toe to toe with the difficult. Your responsibility is to show your disciples that when true faith intersects with God's will, some very dynamic things take place.

11. *Teach your disciples how to witness in their everyday experience.* The most effective form of evangelism for the average person, whom God has placed strategically in the harvest field, is to reach the people around him where he lives, works, and plays. The foremost tool for reaching the world for Christ is the man or woman reaching out in his or her community, neighborhood, and home.

12. *Expect to find opposition to your evangelistic efforts within the religious establishment.* As Jesus reached out to evangelize "sinners," he encountered opposition from the conservative religious community. If God leads you to reach out to a specialized group of people, you may experience resistance from traditionalists, legalists, and weaker brothers. Try to deal with such conflicts with love and patience, but also with determination.

13. *Fellowship with God is the basis for fellowship with others.* This principle was modeled by Jesus and practiced by the early Church. You, too, should establish your disciples in fellowship by teaching them the priority of spending time communicating with God in prayer and Bible study, and

communicating with other believers as you study, pray, eat, sing, play, and reach out together.

14. *The discipler's primary establishing vehicle is the small group.* Jesus spent many months establishing his disciples in God's word, prayer, fellowship, and witnessing. He succeeded so well in this process because he had these men do everything together—in groups. You can bring your disciples together in small groups for Bible study, personal sharing, prayer, and witnessing. Without this vehicle of small groups, we lose the in-depth relationships and the personal touch when our groups are too large.

Part 3

COME AND BE WITH ME:
Equipping

Then [Jesus] said to his disciples, "The harvest is
plentiful but the workers are few. Ask the Lord of
the harvest, therefore, to send out workers into his
harvest field."

Matthew 9:37-38

8
IT IS FOR LIFE

Psychological investigation has yielded the conclusion that a person will not die for something he doesn't believe in. Jesus selected men who, in his judgment, had the kind of conviction necessary for great sacrifice. They were willing not only to *die* for their faith but also to *live* for it.

After they had gone through the process of being established in the basics of ministry, the disciples were ready to actually *be* with Jesus, taking part in the mission of spiritual harvesting. It would not be a four-month stint this time. This time it would be for life! During the "Come and be with me" phase, Jesus' trainees made the critical transition from established disciples to equipped laborers. This period required total investment, for nearly the entire group of men would eventually die for the cause.

As we look in on Jesus now, we see him withdrawing to a

mountain in order to get away from the crowds (Mark 3:13). People closed in on Jesus everywhere he went, both the needy and the antagonistic. "His bitterest enemies followed Him to check on all He was doing and to see if they might trap Him. No doubt the news of bitter criticism brought even more curiosity seekers than before. People follow fame, whether it is favorable or unfavorable."[1]

The common folk followed Jesus primarily because he met their immediate physical need. But Jesus attempted, whenever he could, to wean the people from their superficial following. The "bread of life" teaching proved to be the "acid test." Most of his other disciples abandoned him at that point, but "the twelve" remained with him.

The crowds were both a problem and a possibility. They were a problem in that they presented a vast need to which Jesus could not constantly dedicate himself. The physical limitations of his having a human body made the meeting of every need rather difficult. At the same time, it is indeed God's will to meet all our needs, but he does it according to *his* plan. Jesus had to be in prayer not only to meet the present needs of the crowd, but also to get into motion what would ultimately meet the needs of millions.

Ironically, the same thing that causes growth sometimes kills growth. Jesus was meeting needs, and wherever needs are met, people will beat a path to that door. The overwhelming result, though, was that the crowds became too large for the pressing needs to be adequately met. Sometimes when a pastor does an effective work in a small church, the church grows so large that he is no longer able to deal with the variety of needs that confront him. At that point the church has to acquire more staff. Jesus himself needed more trained staff, and so he went off to pray about who would be his co-laborers.

After spending the entire night in prayer (Luke 6:12),

Jesus "called to him those he wanted, and they came to him. He appointed twelve—designating them apostles—that they might *be with him* . . ." (Mark 3:13-14). These men were the Lord's personal choice; on them rested the future of his kingdom.

The reason for the number *twelve* has been explained by many. Generally, it is determined that twelve is prophetic in character and is related to the twelve tribes of Israel. There is, however, a more practical reason for limiting the number to twelve. It is very difficult to build a close relationship with a thousand, five hundred, or even thirty. Close relationships can be fostered only when people commit themselves to spending time together. In order for some disciples to really *be* with Jesus and learn from him, a large group was out of the question. But the number twelve did indeed grow quite rapidly into the thousands directly after Christ's Resurrection.

As a result of a proper foundation in ministry, the kingdom of God began its ever-expanding multiplication process. By strategically sending out his laborers two-by-two, Jesus guaranteed that the baton of ministry would be passed on through many millennia, until eventually the entire planet will resonate with his good news.

A rag-tag band of misfits

The disciples spent a lot of time with their Master. We can't help but wonder, What was it like to be with Jesus? It was certainly an intimate and ongoing experience. It was intimate because the group was small; ongoing, because the commitment was for life. This personal intimacy afforded Jesus the opportunity to concentrate on each man, to impart his heart for the world into each one.

Jesus had been preaching and casting out demons for eighteen months, and the twelve disciples had witnessed much of that ministry. He now desired that they, too, labor in the harvest field in the same way (Mark 3:14-15). At last the critical transition would take place. Jesus, as the Master Teacher, did not simply cram as much content as possible into the disciples' minds, hoping that somehow they would remember some of it after "graduation."

It is now commonly held that an average person retains only ten percent of what he is taught orally. If that person takes notes and is assisted by visual aids, the retention level is fifty percent. But if, in addition, the person actually partici-pates in *doing* a related activity, the retention level jumps to ninety percent. The disciples were already armed with con-tent. They were established in the word of God, prayer, fellowship, and witnessing. But to become effective in the vital areas of ministry, they would need actual practice.

But what does a person need in particular in order to be ready to actually *labor* in ministry for Jesus? A disciple needs to grow in his *convictions*, to undergo *supervised training experiences* with critique, and to be taught certain *key ministry skills*. It would be three months before Jesus commissioned his disciples to actual laboring. But in the meantime there was much work to be done.

The major difference between a disciple (someone established in God's word, prayer, fellowship, and witness-ing) and a laborer is primarily that the laborer has devel-oped deep *convictions* about reaching the world. Some call it vision; others refer to it as a burden for the lost—a deep, abiding conviction that the world must be reached for God. Jesus would spend much of the next twenty months deepen-ing the conviction of his men. It is one thing to agree that the fields are ripe for harvest, that the harvest is plentiful and the laborers are few, and yet quite another to have a fervor burning in one's heart.

Another difference is that a laborer receives *supervised*

training in the harvest field. He will witness, teach, heal, confront enemies, and then be critiqued by his trainer. Jesus teaches us that without on-the-job training with supervision, true spiritual reproduction will not take place. People learn by *applying* what they have observed and what they have been taught verbally. This kind of pragmatic education calls for one-to-one attention quite often in order to sharpen certain skills and strengthen weaknesses.

A third difference is a laborer's emphasis on *ministry skills.* There are specific skills each laborer must possess in order for a spiritual harvest to take place. The discipler must ask himself the question, What would a laborer need to know and do in order to begin and sustain a ministry? Some of these necessary skills are counseling, evangelizing, and administrating.

As we work our way through the twenty-month "Come and be with me" period, we will be looking for ways in which Jesus *deepened convictions, supervised the disciples' training,* and *developed ministry skills.* He selected twelve men to serve as his laboring team, a team that is essential for meaningful harvesting. A laborer should be able to go out for a sustained period on his own and return with a bounty gleaned from the field. At a certain stage of development, a discipler will, by necessity, select the cream of the crop. He will concentrate on honing the skills of these individuals so that there will be several effective laborers produced, rather than a multitude of disciples still depending on a laboring leader to keep them going.

At some time in your discipling ministry it will be necessary to select a few potential laborers. These people are those through whom you can see the world being reached for the Lord, people who can reproduce your ministry after your departure. Once your decision is made, your total investment as discipler is essential for the successful transition of these people from disciples to laborers. As Jesus demonstrated, time should be given for the cream to rise to the top. It took eighteen months for the curious converts he met right after his baptism to reach this stage of development. Only at that point did Jesus make his decision regarding who the twelve would be.

Usually not much attention is given to the actual list of names in Mark 3:16-19. But let's take a closer look at these men individually. *Simon Peter* was nicknamed "Rock" by Jesus. Peter was an impulsive show-off, the first to exercise faith, and the first to act a fool. He was known for jumping out of boats and walking on water. Peter uttered such memorable statements as, "You are the Christ, the Son of the living God," and, "Even if all fall away on account of you, I never will." This bold fisherman was endowed with extraordinary leadership ability.

James and *John,* sons of Zebedee, were nicknamed "Sons of Thunder" by Jesus. They wanted to call fire down from heaven to smite some uncooperative Samaritans. Apparently aggressiveness ran in the bloodline of these two men. Their dear mother was assertive enough to try to get her boys a special place beside Jesus in his kingdom.

Andrew was commonly referred to as Simon Peter's brother. He was a hard worker, very faithful, someone who could be counted on to give his best under the most difficult circumstances. Andrew was the one who introduced the boy with five loaves and two fish in order to feed the five thousand.

Philip, the analytical type, could be counted on to calculate if a spiritual challenge seemed out of the realm of possibility. He was the resident expert on why certain things could not be done. Later he became an effective evangelist during the early years of the Church.

Bartholomew remains somewhat anonymous. Tradition has it that he was the only one of the twelve with royal blood.

Matthew was formerly a tax collector. His name means "Gift of God." Matthew gave up more earthly wealth than any of the other disciples, but he also gained the most in self-respect.

Thomas was given a bad deal by history by being called "doubting Thomas." But Thomas possessed great courage. On one occasion he called on his fellow disciples, proposing that they should all follow Jesus unto death.

James, the son of Alphaeus, is purported to have preached in Asia and died a martyr's death.

Thaddaeus, also known as Judas son of James, asked Jesus, "Lord, why do you intend to show yourself to us and not to the world?"

Simon the Zealot was a Jewish patriot, the most politically fervent and fanatical of the twelve.

Judas Iscariot is the foremost personal enigma of the New Testament. He served as the treasurer for the men. Although he may have loved the Lord, he didn't seem to have the backbone to suffer for him.

What a kaleidoscope of humanity! A tax collector (Matthew) and a tax hater (Simon the Zealot); the impulsive Peter and the quiet, analytical Philip; the ambitious James and John beside the more reserved Andrew and Bartholomew; a man who was willing to die (Thomas) and a man who just couldn't take it (Judas). The genius of Jesus' choice of these men is that when we look at them, it is like looking in the mirror. When I look in the mirror, I see the impulsiveness of Peter, the apprehension of Andrew, the skepticism of Thomas, the calculating doubt of Philip, and even the mutinous leanings of Judas.

You see, this list of men is not meant to be held up as a model of perfection. Rather, these disciples are a promise— a promise to you and me that God can and will use us! We are just like these men, and they are like us. As we look at the people we are discipling, we can see the Peters—so excited, filled with grand ideas, often making mistakes, but without whom the work wouldn't go very far. We see the Andrews— knowing that they want to follow the Lord, but not knowing if they are up to it, and yet giving it all they've got anyhow. There are the Philips, who don't think they can afford to take the time off to become effective, and yet they are willing to die. The Thomases doubt whether anything will come of all this laboring business, but they will go along just to see. And the Judases say, "I've heard there is a better deal with another group; the requirements aren't as stiff."

Jesus called all twelve to be with him. This rag-tag band of misfits turned the world upside-down, most of them dying as martyrs. What set them apart was that they were attracted to Jesus and they weren't afraid to show it. A discipler should always look for those who are willing to come apart from the crowd, desiring to make their lives count for Christ.

Indeed, men were his method, and from this point forward in his ministry, Jesus' focus would be the training of the twelve. As the Crucifixion drew closer, Jesus spent more and more time with them. The twelve were with him almost constantly.

The decision concerning what comes first in training disciples is a difficult but important one. The way we begin sets the pace for subsequent training. In this third phase of training, the first thing Jesus did was to sit his men down to teach them the backbone of the believer's lifestyle. This extended teaching is commonly referred to as the Sermon on the Mount (Matthew 5-7). In this teaching Jesus presented his men with a mental framework for their theology. The ethics expounded here are the backbone for a person's interior life, a foundation for responding to the stimuli of the world.

There on that mountain, Jesus explained to his men

that *attitude* forms the basis for success in ministry. Christian service is a vast and rigorous challenge, and yet also a potential danger. The burden of ministry can erode ideas, destroy vision, and cause the eternal optimist to be a disillusioned pessimist. Thus our inner perspective is vital as we face the hardships of front-line ministry.

As we encounter the struggles of ministry, we find dogged resistance from our Satanic enemy. He wants to turn our challenge into a defeat.

Furthermore, ministry is tough because we are working with people, or, more graphically, *sheep*. Isaiah told us that we are all like sheep; we tend to go our own way.

But in spite of all the obstacles, God keeps calling disciples to labor in the harvest field. If we are to labor effectively with joy and good emotional health, we must handle these pressures with spiritual fortitude.

In this mountainside sermon, Jesus told his men what kind of people they needed to be in order not only to *survive* ministry but also to enjoy it and prosper in it. In this profound teaching, the Master emphasized humility, sincerity, righteousness, mercy, sensitivity, reconciliation, integrity, and love—all qualities necessary for his followers. And then he concluded his message with an interesting metaphor about two ways to build a house.

> "Everyone who hears these words of mine and puts them into practice is like a wise man who built his house on the rock. The rain came down, the streams rose, and the winds blew and beat against the house; yet it did not fall, because it had its foundation on the rock. But everyone who hears these words of mine and does not put them into practice is like a foolish man who built his house on sand. The rain came down, the streams rose, and the winds blew and beat against that house, and it fell with a great crash." (Matthew 7:24-27)

The lesson here is that someone who wants to labor for the Lord needs to practice what he knows to be true. Furthermore, if the laborer desires his ministry to endure, he must have the *character* and the *skills* to effectively labor. He must be like the wise man, building his ministry on the solid rock of Christ himself. The foolish man builds his ministry on other foundations that have been offered by the world. As the winds of difficulty and deep waters of struggle come, the superficial laborer will fold. The person of character, however, who possesses the right inner qualities, whose life penetrates into the world, will labor long and effectively for the King.

As they descended that mountain with their Master that day, the disciples at last knew the cost of discipleship. They realized that they could not spend the rest of their days sitting at the feet of the Master continually drinking it in. No, they were indeed called to go on their own, out into the harvest fields. It would not be a quick, random foray. This time it would require great dedication and skill. This time it was for life.

Footnotes:

1. Carl Wilson, *With Christ in the School of Disciple Building* (Grand Rapids: Zondervan, 1976), page 142.

9
A LABOR OF LOVE

Even though the average person has two ears, sometimes that's just not enough to really hear. Often Jesus found himself talking to people who were "ever hearing but never understanding" (Mark 4:12). The crowds quite readily accepted his miraculous healings, and yet many of these same people would not accept his message.

As the twelve disciples were beginning to learn the fundamentals of laboring in the spiritual harvest fields, they developed a very unique sense of hearing that enabled them to understand spiritual truth when they heard it. When their Master delivered the Sermon on the Mount to an awestruck crowd, he was not just giving out casual advice or theological facts. He was giving them the living word of God. Jesus' mountainside message contained the radical call to go beyond the right legalistic *motions* of the Law, focusing instead on the right *attitude* within. He emphasized that the key is *love* (Matthew 5:43-48, 22:36-40).

The kind of laboring the Master was teaching his twelve men was very special, for it was a labor of love. Jesus really cared about people.

> When he saw the crowds, he had compassion on them, because they were harassed and helpless, like sheep without a shepherd. Then he said to his disciples, "The harvest is plentiful but the workers are few. Ask the Lord of the harvest, therefore, to send out workers into his harvest field." (Matthew 9:36-38)

This was the second time Jesus mentioned the harvest to his disciples. The first occasion was at the close of the introductory ministry exposure, the "Come and see" phase. He had, at that time, left them thinking about this pressing need for laborers to be sent into the harvest field. Now, at another crucial transition in the training of the twelve, he was once again expressing the concern of his heart. The Master was describing both the need and the solution. The need was *harvesting,* the solution, *workers.*

A striking feature of Jesus' character is illuminated here—he felt *compassion* for people. Compassion gives birth to the meeting of needs. It multiplies itself spiritually in other people. Any laborer worth his salt will be periodically overwhelmed with the massive, worthy need that exists all around him and the gigantic effort it takes to meet that need.

Jesus empathized emotionally with the need of the people. They were truly a "harassed" mass of humanity (Matthew 9:36). The Master's inner being pained him, for he fully understood their plight. The perfect Man could not detach himself from the anguish of unmet need. Jesus not only understood the full theological implications (the people's lost spiritual state) but he also fully identified with the common pain of being human in an inhuman world.

The nature of the harvest field

According to Jesus, a plentiful harvest was being neglected. The solution was workers or laborers to go into the harvest field. One means of getting laborers into that field is *praying* (Matthew 9:38). Another even more direct means is *going*.

The time had arrived for Jesus to call his men to action. Jesus summoned the twelve, commissioned them, and began sending them out two by two in six teams (Mark 6:7). This was to be their "field" education. But before they departed, he told a parable describing the nature of the harvest field they would be entering.

> "Listen! A farmer went out to sow his seed. As he was scattering the seed, some fell along the path, and the birds came and ate it up. Some fell on rocky places, where it did not have much soil. It sprang up quickly, because the soil was shallow. But when the sun came up, the plants were scorched, and they were withered because they had no root. Other seed fell among thorns, which grew up and choked the plants, so that they did not bear grain. Still other seed fell on good soil. It came up, grew and produced a crop, multiplying thirty, sixty, or even a hundred times. . . ."
>
> "The farmer sows the word. Some people are like the seed along the path, where the word is sown. As soon as they hear it, Satan comes and takes away the word that was sown in them. Others, like the seed sown on rocky places, hear the word and at once receive it with joy. But since they have no root, they last only a short time. When trouble or persecution comes because of the word, they quickly fall away. Still others, like seed sown among thorns, hear the word; but the worries of this life, the deceitfulness of wealth and the desires for

other things come in and choke the word, making it unfruitful. Others, like seed sown on good soil, hear the word, accept
it, and produce a crop—thirty, sixty or even a hundred times
what was sown." (Mark 4:3-8, 14-20)

This is a parable about a laborer out in the harvest field.
What should a laborer expect when he steps out into the
world to proclaim the word of God? Will most people like
what he says, or will the majority reject the message? Should I
be discouraged if people oppose what I stand for? Must I
keep pressing on even if no one responds positively? These
are the obvious questions the laborer asks as he contem-
plates ministry.

I have wondered (from a discouraged posture, I must
confess) what happens to all the preaching and teaching
that goes on, especially mine. There is virtually a flood of
Christian sermons, Bible studies, television and radio programs, tapes, and literature out there in American society.
Millions of words are spoken and written every day by
Christians. But the question we have to ask ourselves is, Does
all this Christian communication really make any difference?

One preacher was frustrated with his efforts to convert
a stubborn parishioner. Since his church was small, the
pastor had an opportunity for close contact with this man.
Every week the unconverted member would listen to the
message, and on the way out he would say, "Preacher, you
really got them today," never even considering that the
sermon might have had some possible application to his
own life.

One snowy Sunday morning, it just so happened that
this man was the only one able to get to church. The pastor
took this as providential, and so he preached his heart out,
eloquently zeroing in on the need for salvation. At the close
of the service, the typically blasé man shook hands with the

pastor and said, "Preacher, if they had been here today, you really would've got 'em." Now that's frustration!

It is true, many parishioners blatantly ignore the proclaimed word of God, yet hang on every syllable of the evening news. Statements doled out in sermonic form are casually dismissed, but the same thing said one-on-one would cause offense. Sometimes it is true that lack of interest in God's word is due to dull preaching, and certainly there is no excuse for that. But the Bible itself describes an even greater impediment to communication—"dull hearing" (Hebrews 5:11).

Many a frustrated speaker has expressed his puzzlement: "Can't they hear what I'm saying? They have two good ears, don't they?" Jesus himself stated several times, "He who has ears to hear, let him hear," implying that merely having the equipment to hear does not guarantee understanding. He was speaking of some inner spiritual ear that is tuned to the voice of God. Jesus indicated, in his parable of the sower, that although there are many different kinds of people, there is only one kind who will respond to God's word positively with lasting results. Such people possess a special sensitivity of spiritual hearing.

As we study this parable, there are three general factors about parables that we need to consider: first, the setting; second, the symbols; and third, the meaning of the symbols and their application to life. A thorough analysis of this particular parable should give us a good understanding of what a laborer for Jesus has to encounter.

The setting—Jesus was there in a boat, just off the shore. Crowds were gathered around him; the Pharisees were watching and waiting. Not much had changed—except for one thing. In a sense this was a dramatic change. He was now teaching in parables.

A *parable* is an earthly story with a heavenly meaning,

which gives an immediate impression. The Greek word *parabolē* indicates something that is placed alongside something else, usually for comparison. A parable is a story that is easily understood because it applies to life as we see it every day. Daily, mundane activities are placed *alongside* corresponding spiritual realities.

Jesus' most profound teachings were word pictures. He carved out large chunks of truth from everyday life. In the case of this parable, he chose familiar agricultural symbols: sowing, growth, and harvest. The lessons of this parable were specially tailored to his disciples' learning needs. Even though they were puzzled at first, the Master explained that they were gifted by God to understand the vital truths contained within his parabolic teachings (Mark 4:11).

> With many similar parables Jesus spoke the word to them, as much as they could understand. He did not say anything to them without using a parable. But when he was alone with his own disciples, he explained everything. (Mark 4:33-34)

Jesus' reason for using so many parables can be understood clearly in the context of the growing resistance to his ministry on the part of the Jewish legalists. The parable phase of Jesus' ministry was essential for at least three reasons.

The first is given in Matthew 13:13: "This is why I speak to [the people] in parables: 'Though seeing, they do not see; though hearing, they do not hear or understand.'" Jesus desired to continue teaching his disciples, but in a way that the hardhearted and the dull of hearing would not be able to understand. Until this phase of his teaching, Jesus had addressed himself largely to Israel's religious establishment. Now that they had totally rejected him as their Messiah, he turned away from them.

Second, Jesus wanted only the spiritually hungry to understand his teaching. Those having spiritual ears to hear and eyes to see would comprehend his truths.

Third, he didn't want to give the Pharisees any more information than was necessary concerning his future plans, for they used all such information in an attempt to abort his ministry efforts. Because they rejected his Messianic representative, God gave them a spiritual unawareness. Israel thus developed a spirit of stupor, a further hardening of its already hardened heart. Jesus simply would not play games with those who were not interested in his work, for he was playing for the highest stakes of all: mankind's eternal destiny.

The symbols—A parable is normally packed with visual images that represent certain spiritual counterparts. In the case of this parable of the sower, there are three primary symbols.

(1) The *seed* represents the word of God (Mark 4:3,14). A seemingly small and insignificant seed, given the right conditions, produces the mighty redwoods of California, the beautiful palms of Florida, and the stately oaks of the Midwest. When a seed is given enough time, it can cause a sidewalk to crack, a foundation to split, or a patio to break. A few years ago I stood beside a redwood tree 270 feet high and 6,300 tons heavy, an arboreal giant that came from a seed weighing three-thousandth of an ounce.

The Holy Spirit provides the right conditions for the seed of the word of God to come alive. When this happens, it is nothing short of revolutionary. It saves broken families, troubled businesses, and crushed churches. The word of God turns cannibals into missionaries and criminals into evangelists. The word is a living, spiritual seed (1 Peter 1:23).

(2) The *sower* is the one who delivers the word to others. Whether a polished sermon or a simple witness, a sentence

or a song, if it contains Scripture it qualifies as sowing. It is the responsibility of every Christian to be a sower of the word, to be responsive to the opportunities that come our way. Much like the seed, God's word has the ability to survive the mistakes of those who handle it.

(3) The *soil* represents the human heart. Soil and seed are made for each other. When they come together, wonderful things can transpire. This is the case then the word of God and the human heart come together.

The meaning—In first-century Palestine, sowing preceded plowing. The sower would indiscriminately scatter the seed on top of the ground. He did not know, while sowing, what the exact condition of the soil happened to be. Even after plowing, only a few hints of the soil's condition were evident.

When one is sowing the seed of the word of God, he cannot know for certain the heart of the hearer. Just as the sower is not directly responsible for the harvest results after the seed is in the soil, likewise the laborer is not responsible for the spiritual results after the word is delivered to a person's heart. The laborer simply sows in the power of the Holy Spirit, leaving the results in the hands of God.

Jesus gave his men invaluable insight into the four basic kinds of hearts (the soils) to whom they would be preaching.

(1) The *hardened* heart:

"Some people are like seed along the path, where the word is sown. As soon as they hear it, Satan comes and takes away the word that was sown in them." (Mark 4:15)

Picture in your mind a well-worn path, beaten down by many travelers so that the ground is hard. The seed lies on the surface, easy prey for birds. The disciples could easily identify this type as the Pharisees—no penetration, no understanding. Like the fool of the Proverbs, they are hard-ened and insensitive, unwilling to listen to wise counsel, ever bending and twisting the truth. Satan easily comes in and snatches the word of God from them before any good can come of it.

(2) The *shallow* heart:

> "Others, like seed sown on rocky places, hear the word and at once receive it with joy. But since they have no root, they last only a short time. When trouble or persecution comes because of the word, they quickly fall away." (Mark 4:16-17)

After the farmer plows, he discovers that some seed has fallen on shallow soil, not deep enough for the seed to take root (verses 5-6). At first the seed sprouts up, and there is apparent growth and joy. But it is not lasting; the sun scorches it because it has no root. People who hear the word of God and immediately get emotionally high are often experienc-ing joy without thought. Perhaps they were pressured into making a premature decision. There was some immediate spiritual relief, but in the long run it proved to be only temporary relief.

When the difficulties of life bear down like the heat of the sun, a superficial commitment begins to wither and die. It is a matter of human nature to make quick decisions that we later cannot live up to. However, anyone who wants to follow Jesus should first stop to count the long-term cost of discipleship. A decision to follow Jesus should be a sincere pledge from the heart *and* the mind.

Beware the impulsive, shallow heart among Christians and non-Christians alike. Jesus said that people will make decisions to follow him and then drop out. We should expect some people to say (quite sincerely, in fact), "I want to be a disciple; I desire to labor; I will give up my life" . . . and later they disappear from sight. The experienced laborer knows that attrition is a real part of ministry, one that should not discourage him.

(3) The *crowded* heart:

"Still others, like seed sown among thorns, hear the word; but the worries of this life, the deceitfulness of wealth and the desires for other things come in and choke the word, making it unfruitful." (Mark 4:18-19)

Some soil is soft and has depth, but it is impure. Thorns and weeds choke out the life. The strangulation of spiritual life apparently takes place in three different ways.

First, there are "the worries of this life." Anxiety concerning our future, our work, our health, food, and clothing can preoccupy a person, rendering him useless. Some people become so overwhelmed with anxiety that God is squeezed out of any meaningful part of their lives.

Second, certain people are quite easily enticed by the material possibilities of life. Many people immerse themselves in the pursuit of pleasure and wealth. But riches always promise more than they can deliver. Even the rich can come up empty.

Third, many people are plagued by an intense, perpetual desire for something more. A restlessness born out of insecurity and spiritual alienation gives rise to longings that demand satisfaction. Cravings for prestige, power, and recognition can be powerful inner motives causing many people to ignore the priorities of Scripture and to eventually abandon the cause of Christ. God is thus crowded out by the world.

A gardener must not only love flowers: he must also hate weeds. Weeds grow naturally; they don't require any special care. As weeds thrive, they crowd out the flowers the gardener has planted. Sometimes it is difficult for serious laborers to tell the difference between the flowers and the weeds. Often time alone is necessary to show whether the plant growing in someone's heart is a flower or a weed. For if the right kind of "fruit" is not borne, then we know that true salvation has probably not taken place (4:19).

The proof of salvation is not a quick emotional response or a temporary faith that evaporates at the first sign of difficulty. The proof, according to Jesus, is fruit. "By their fruit you will recognize them" (Matthew 7:20). The explicit statement concerning this third soil is that no fruit is produced, substantiating that indeed this is only a worldly facsimile of rebirth.

(4) The *good* heart:

> "Others, like seed sown on good soil, hear the word, accept it, and produce a crop—thirty, sixty or even a hundred times what was sown." (Mark 4:20)

All the signs of salvation are present in the good soil: growth, increase, and a large bounty. The believing heart *will* bear fruit. Therefore, the simple way to examine faith is by looking for the presence of fruit. Unlike the hardened heart, the good heart is receptive; unlike the impulsive heart, it understands; and unlike the crowded heart, there is singleness of purpose.

A major lesson to be learned from the parable is that we should not be overly concerned about the indicated response or lack of it when we are proclaiming the gospel. We cannot force the response. The laborer is simply to share Christ in the power of the Holy Spirit, leaving the results with God. The sower sows the word of God; the hearing and the responding are outside his responsibility.

Yet another truth that surfaces is that good soil will

multiply fruit. Today's convert is tomorrow's disciple and next year's laborer and leader. The spiritual multiplication through the effort of laborers is God's perfect plan for reaching the world.

Howard Ball, president of Churches Alive, speaks often of the "convoy mentality," an unfortunate syndrome among Christians. This is the false notion that a church shouldn't move ahead on a project until everyone agrees. Rarely does everyone agree! The unfortunate result of official hesitation is that paralysis sets in, and thus much effort is wasted by leaders trying to get the non-movers moving. The grievous consequence is that the church's lifestyle becomes dictated by the disobedient. Leaders get tied up with the problem-people, and eventually get fed up with leadership.

The laborer must try to select those who are willing to move. Although he must initially distribute the seed of God's word rather indiscriminately, eventually the laborer must launch out into the deep waters of ministry, leaving behind those who are not willing to go. Jesus himself turned away from the hardened, unbelieving ecclesiastical leadership and from all others whose lives reflected the first three soils.

By using parables in his teaching, the Master began to concentrate on only those with hungry hearts. He left behind him the hardened, the impulsive, and the worldly—those who were not interested in seriously pursuing the kingdom of God. Anyone who labors in the harvest field of the world inevitably encounters outright resistance and rejections as Jesus did from the hardened legalists. Sometimes the resistance to God's word is really obvious, and yet other times it is more subtle, requiring time to show the true soil-state. But the one who labors must single-mindedly persevere in his task, entrusting the harvest to God.

10
BECOMING MORE
LIKE THE MASTER

Trying something for the very first time is often both exciting and frightening. No matter how much advance training precedes that solo flight, the value of the experience itself far surpasses all preparation. Apprenticeship is very important, but there comes a natural time when the student graduates and goes out to confront the world on his own, putting into practice all that he has learned.

When Jesus gathered his twelve men together to send them out into the harvest field, it was much like a parent sending Junior off on his own. Even though they would be returning eventually for some post-graduate studies, this was the disciples' first independent ministry venture.

If spiritual multiplication is to take place, converts must mature into established disciples who must then ripen into equipped laborers. These laborers in turn need to be able to nurture and train other disciples through this same growth process. The Great Commission hinges on this very process (Matthew 28:19-20).

There is now in process a major shift in many churches of the Western world—a shift from clergy-centered ministry to a ministry of laymen equipped for service. This change in the Western world is gradually taking place all around us. Christian leaders are lovingly but firmly leading the Church out of the misconceptions and mistakes of the past to the proper scriptural pattern intended by God. The goal of many individual churches is to transform a congregation of spectators being led by a minister into an army of ministers being led by a pastor.

Out on their own

As we look at Jesus instructing his twelve men before they went off to minister in the harvest field, we see the model Disciplemaker. He knew what was most important in the spiritual weaning process. The proper releasing of a child, employee, or disciple is crucial. The assignment must be challenging enough to allow them to be tested to their limit but not beyond it. The releasing should be a gradual process.

Teaching my son to ride a bicycle was a progressive experience. He sat proudly atop his new bike, securely balanced as I walked beside him with one hand on the back of the seat and the other on the handle bars. Then a few days later I only had a hand on the back of the seat as I pushed the bike and whispered encouragement into his ear. Walking progressed to running.

Finally, the day came when I determined that I would run alongside the bike as usual, but at a certain moment let go of the bike altogether. As I let go, he kept on riding just as though I were still holding on. The instant he discovered he was on his own, he screamed and crashed. And yet he realized that he had made it a few feet by himself, and so within a few minutes he was joyfully riding all over the parking lot without any assistance.

Jesus released the disciples in much the same way as I finally released my son's bicycle. In a similar manner, he was sending them out now on local missions, letting them know that he was close by to help them if needed. This by no means represented the final releasing to full responsibility. It was simply the initial solo flight by the twelve.

Jesus gave his men precise instructions concerning this first solo session. Within this ministry briefing, we find four broad training principles that can be useful in our twentieth century approach to equipping laborers.

1. *Send them two by two.*

There are several reasons for sending laborers in pairs rather than in trios or quartets. The smaller duo gives each person the opportunity to fully utilize his gifts. When two people work on a project, each one is required to do a diversity of jobs.

These twelve men had been watching Jesus for over sixteen months. They were bursting with information and untested knowledge. But they needed the freedom to translate theory into action. They would have to do their own thinking, planning, praying, trusting, and preaching. Without the luxury of turning around to ask Jesus for advice, they would learn fast how to think on their feet.

A team of two offers the positive opportunity for a personal closeness. It is much easier to develop a trusting relationship with just one other person. A team of three or more may bring about competition for intimacy or the chance of two turning on one. When two are out in the field by themselves, they tend to rely on each other rather than competing with each other.

Another positive characteristic is the accountability

factor. A man alone is open to many more temptations than he is when he has someone to whom he must answer and be held accountable. Generally, this accountability is not something that is clearly articulated; it simply exists because these two people are close together in the ministry.

2. *Give them authority.*

Never ask someone to start a task unless you have given him the authority to complete the job. A laborer needs a detailed description of the job he is to do, plus the equipment and the knowhow. But most of all he must have the necessary authority. There is nothing more frustrating than giving your best to something that, in the end, is futile because you did not possess the authority to successfully complete the task.

Jesus made sure that full authority was given to the disciples; when confronted with a demon, they could respond in the same manner as their Teacher (Mark 6:7). Confidence is crucial in ministry; having authority breeds confidence, and confidence enhances performance.

3. *Specify the audience.*

Jesus clearly instructed his men, "Do not go among the Gentiles or enter any town of the Samaritans. Go rather to the lost sheep of Israel" (Matthew 10:5-6). Jesus had a plan dictating that the Jewish population be the first to hear the good news of the kingdom of God. The Father's agenda determined this approach. Promises rooted in the Old Testament required that Israel be offered the kingdom of God along with their promised Messiah. It was a matter of first things first. Thus, the disciples were to assist in the divine agenda.

The theological and cultural barriers between Jew and Gentile were much too great for the twelve to cross on their maiden tour. When a novice is trying out his ministry wings for the first time, you shouldn't set him up to fail by placing insurmountable barriers in his path. Healing the sick and casting out demons they could handle, but offering a Samaritan (a half-breed Jew) the kingdom—well, that's another story.

People in the early stages of learning should never have too many options confronting them. If these men had been sent out to preach to everyone who crossed their path, they would have been easily sidetracked by the enemy. Because they had such specific instructions regarding who they should speak to, it was far more difficult for Satan to hinder their work.

4. *Clarify the objective.*

Exactly what message should this particular audience of first-century Jews hear? Jesus told his men, "As you go, preach this message: 'The kingdom of heaven is near'" (Matthew 10:7). Here was a unique message for a unique people, a message that only a Jew would understand or be interested in.

Having a specific message for a specific target group simplifies the ministry task. Laborers should be able to present the gospel with clarity so that there is no confusing of the issues. Training all laborers in the same method is suggested at the outset. This way the trainer is sure that everyone knows at least one way to effectively share the gospel. Other methods are fine, too, if they are appropriate, but the discipler's responsibility is to ensure that everyone can effectively share his own faith.

Newly-called workers should not be expected to answer all questions and objections to the gospel. Some believe that if a Christian cannot explain every cult, answer every objection, and debate every philosophical question, then he is not ready to witness to others regarding his faith. Not true. But it is vitally important that we know quite thoroughly what we believe, for only then will we be able to refute error. As a person gains experience in presenting the gospel message, he tends to study the Scriptures and other materials more and more in order to answer the questions he has been confronted with. The Christian has the advantage of possessing a supernatural message that, when faithfully used, will do its appointed work (Isaiah 55:11).

Further instructions from the Master to the laborers included specifics on subjects such as healing the sick, raising the dead, delivering the demon-possessed, hints on how to finance ministry, suggestions on clothing, and guidelines for finding lodging (Matthew 10:8-14, Mark 6:8-11). Hostility and hospitality are both mentioned, with hints on how to handle each. One gets the impression that Jesus wanted his men to experience total dependence on him as they ministered without any backup system or support.

With a sense of newfound confidence and accomplishment, the twelve men ministered as they were asked to do. "They went out and preached that people should repent. They drove out many demons and anointed many sick people with oil and healed them" (Mark 6:12-13). Here they were for the first time, out on their own and laboring. Jesus had equipped them sufficiently for a first mission.

When training laborers for a mission, a discipler should be as committed to detailed planning and instruction as Jesus was. Jesus gave his men the details and specifics. He covered all the bases, left nothing of substance out, and did everything possible to ensure that his men would be successful. On-the-job training must be thorough, progressive, and well-rehearsed. The disciples had watched Jesus often, and so they knew what he meant when he said, Preach the message, heal people, cast out demons. They had seen him do these things, which made them far more capable of doing them.

Later in his ministry, Jesus sent out seventy-two of his

other disciples two by two into the harvest field. They eventually returned to tell Jesus all that had been accomplished on their journeys (Luke 10:17). Accountability is indeed essential in effective training. Continuous review and application were woven throughout the Master's "Come and be with me" training period. His Transfiguration, the feeding of the five thousand, the stilling of the storm, and his walking on water were all lessons discussed by Jesus and his men.

A person who is just learning the ropes of laboring not only *needs* supervision but in most cases *desires* it. Because of our fallen human nature, when we are given an assignment we need to give an account of our experience. A vital part of leadership is the assisting of trainees in learning and improving skills. As a leader, I would be sinning against the ones I train and those my trainees touch if I neglect to supervise.

I meet weekly with laborers who are training disciples in small-group settings. These laborers fill out reports, answer questions, and share their joys and concerns. A lot of troubleshooting is done in this context, and together we learn from each other's successes and failures. If there were no meetings and no accountability, the quality of disciple-making would be greatly reduced.

The leaders of the world system enjoy domineering those under their influence (Mark 10:42-43). The Christian leader, on the other hand, lovingly leads, corrects, and guides in harmony with the Holy Spirit's ministry to other believers. When Jesus called his men together, they shared with excitement their many experiences. Those discussions provided an integral part of training just as important as the tour itself.

Rowing against the wind

As we look back over the three distinct phases of the Master's training of his men, we see that the disciples had traversed a long way. During the first period ("Come and see"), the men were just curious converts, gradually exposed by the Master to the nature of ministry. The second stage ("Come and follow me") was a foundational time for Jesus to establish his fledgling disciples, immersing them in Scripture study, prayer, witnessing, and fellowship.

But at the point of the third phase ("Come and be with me"), the twelve disciples were ready to embark out on their own, crossing the bridge from an unexplored commitment to an active responsibility. They were no longer just spectator-*disciples*; they were becoming productive *disciplemakers*.

In the remaining time prior to his date with destiny, Jesus concentrated on deepening the convictions and sharpening the ministry skills of his men. Now, after they returned from their solo tour of ministry, his twelve laborers were ready for some final, weighty field-experience with their Trainer.

We look in on Jesus now as he listens to the ministry report of his men. But things are rather confusing because of all the people pressing in on them (Mark 6:30-31). So Jesus suggests that they go off in a boat together in order to have some solitude and rest. However, they arrive on a shore on another portion of the Sea of Galilee only to discover that the relentless crowd has hastily preceded them to their hideaway (Mark 6:32-34). This spiritually hungry mob actually hurried around the sea by land many extra miles and was waiting on the other side when Jesus and the twelve arrived.

Many leaders would have cried out in exasperation at this point, "Won't these people give me a moment to myself?" He certainly could have protested. When I want some privacy I can go home, lock the door, take the phone off the hook, and retreat from the demands of time and need. But Jesus "had compassion on them."

Compassion is the quality that makes such things as courage, hard work, discipling, planning, and skill meaningful. All the ability in Christendom falls short as a substitute for compassion and caring about human need. God doesn't bless gifts, personalities, and skills; he simply uses them. God blesses the character within us when our hearts are tender with compassion.

Jesus didn't just pat the people on the head and meet their immediate physical and emotional needs. We are told that he began to teach them. Jesus is committed to the *truth* because, in his own words, the truth alone will set us free (John 8:32). Wonderful experiences will not set us free. Platitudes, pop psychology, and warm emotions will not set us free. Only truth will provide a permanent solution for our needs, and that truth is embodied in Jesus (John 14:6).

As it got quite late in the day, the disciples suggested to the Master another attempt at finding a hideaway from the crowd. But Jesus knew that all these people were getting hungry. The disciples recommended to their Master that he send the people away to find their own food. But Jesus had another solution in mind. "He answered, 'You give them something to eat'" (Mark 6:37). But they told him that buying bread for so many people would cost too much. Jesus then asked them, "How many loaves do you have? Go and see."

At this point the disciples started looking in various lunch sacks, and soon found a lad with a lunch of five loaves of bread and two fish. As Andrew handed the lad's lunch over to Jesus, the Master was waiting for those words of faith he longs to hear from all his followers. But the words didn't come. The words of Andrew were instead loaded with skepticism: "Here is a boy with five small barley loaves and two small fish, but how far will they go among so many?" (John 6:9).

How many of us have a little of Andrew in us? We desire

to do our best, but our best is so small in light of the massive
need around us. We think our little gift to the Lord's work—
our little time, talent, or contribution—won't make a difference. But this is not what Jesus wants to hear from his
laborers. What he desires to hear is, "This is all we have,
Lord. But now *you* take over. Here, Lord, this is all we have,
but that's all you ever ask. You can make something out of it,
Lord, because a little is a lot in your hands."

I have heard many Christian leaders imply in a round-
about way that Jesus is holding out on their churches. They
say, "If only we had more mature leaders in our church . . . if
only we had better singers and pianists . . . if only we could
have more staff . . . if only we had more wealthy people . . .
then our organization could really grow and develop."

What a faithless attitude! Christ hasn't shortchanged
his people. His Church has everything it needs right now.
Every gift, every talent, every dollar needed presently resides
in his Church. This is why discipleship is so critical: because
the untapped resources in our churches reside in the undis-
cipled members of our congregations.

What Jesus is asking from his disciples is that we say,
when faced with the impossible situation, "Here, Lord—I
don't know how to do this, but you do. This is all I have; you
take it and multiply it thirtyfold, a hundredfold, or a thou-
sandfold. Jesus quietly but effectively performed the miracle
of feeding five thousand. He gave each of the twelve his own
full basket of leftovers (Mark 6:43). One can only imagine
the astounded look on Andrew's face as he stood there with
his basket; Peter, basking with pride in his Lord; and Judas,
thinking, I wonder how much we could get for this in town.

Finally the disciples were convinced; they had learned
their lesson on faith; they would never doubt Jesus again,
right? Wrong. Certainly we would think that Jesus had finished off any doubt in the disciples' hearts. But Jesus knew

that they needed at least one more mind-boggling assignment on this long, arduous day.

Because teaching came naturally for Jesus, he recognized opportunities for learning encounters quickly and
acted on them without hesitation. This is an enviable trait for
any leader of disciples. Jesus led his men into their next test
of faith with a simple directive. "Immediately Jesus made his
disciples get into the boat and go on ahead of him to
Bethsaida, while he dismissed the crowd. After leaving them,
he went into the hills to pray" (Mark 6:45-46).

Jesus was putting his disciples out to sea in a storm for a
learning experience. But he placed them there while, like a
protective parent, he kept them within arm's reach. He was
on the land alone, praying; they were on the sea together,
struggling with their oars against the force of the wind (verse
48). There they were, between three and six in the morning,
digging in furiously with the blast of the storm in their faces.
Talk about discouragement!

There are many occasions when laborers work very
hard, and yet they get nowhere. We find ourselves "out at
sea" alone, struggling, fighting against various elements of
life: financial, relational, physical—it makes no difference.
These are the tests of our faith.

There on the stormy Galilean Sea, Jesus wanted to
know if the twelve had learned anything from the feeding of
the five thousand. Jesus decided to go to them—walking on
the water! Interestingly, the text tells us that he was about to
walk right by them. We could chalk this up to Jesus' great
sense of humor; perhaps he would have kept on going if
they hadn't asked him for help. I think Jesus wanted to see if
they would look for him in the storm. Would he be invited
into the boat or would they let him walk by?

When they finally saw their Master, they mistook him
for a ghost and cried out in fear. But quickly he reassured

them that it was he and told them not to be afraid. When Peter realized that Jesus was walking on water, he decided to request, in so many words, "Lord, let *me* try that, too!" (Matthew 14:28). The quality that set Peter apart from most of the other disciples was his adventurous faith. As Peter stepped out of the boat and looked into the eyes of Jesus, he must have said, "Wow, this is great!" But then, "when he saw the wind, he was afraid and, beginning to sink, cried out, 'Lord, save me!'"(14:30).

Peter saw the wind and waves, which to us represent the difficult circumstances and challenges of life. Peter began to sink because he was suffering from the paralysis of human analysis. The rationalizing conclusion that "This can't be done," and the fatalistic idea that "I'm not supposed to do something this special" overcame Peter. Our Satanic enemy and the world both stir up many winds and waves that would serve as threats to our effectiveness. But if we keep our eyes on Jesus, we can prevail over adversity.

Jesus rescued the sinking Peter, but added this rebuke: "You of little faith, why did you doubt?" (14:31). God wants us to keep our eyes on Jesus in order to prevent us from being engulfed by our circumstances, especially at those times when we're rowing against the wind. This is our challenge of faith.

As the Master got into the boat, the storm ceased. His disciples were so awed that they worshiped him. Apparently they had gained no insight from the incident of the loaves and fish, for their hearts had been hardened (Mark 6:51-52). Their minds were not hardened in the same sense as the minds of the Pharisees. Rather, the disciples were unable, in their state of mind, to put together the pieces in the puzzle of Jesus' identity *in relation to their lives.*

Never assume that awe-inspiring moments automatically lead to lessons permanently learned. Oftentimes we remember the event and miss the lesson. One of the more frustrating moments for the discipler is when the disciples deliver all the right theology verbally, only to flunk miserably when theological theory proves to be off the mark in real life. It is easy to believe that God can do anything. But for *me?* Here and now? Well, that's another thing.

The deepening of convictions goes on and on when God is part of the process. Even Jesus, the perfect Teacher, needed twenty months to ready these laborers for leadership. *Repeated experience* will move the pieces of the puzzle around enough in the disciple's head so that one day the pieces will actually fit. Toward the end of a laborer's training period, he ought to be checked to see if he has the philosophical pieces of the puzzle together. Jesus wanted to know if his men had related his ability to feed five thousand to the meeting of their need amid the storm. He wanted them to recognize that they needed to weave him into the fabric of their lives, relating him to every portion of existence.

The laborer needs to understand theologically and philosophically what is needed to reach the world. He needs to know what Scripture teaches concerning the person of God and the salvation of man, the nature of ministry, the need for making disciples and calling laborers into the harvest fields, and how to train those laborers in order to prepare them for leadership. He needs to know how to start and maintain a ministry with Christ in charge. The philosophical aspect relates to methods of executing his theology. In other words, the laborer should be able to explain why making disciples forms the foundation for all other ministry. He should understand that a church should not consider making disciples just one of its ministries. Rather, a church should consider itself a discipling center. If anything a church does is not contributing to the making of disciples, then it should be closely scrutinized.

If a laborer is turned loose on his own without having the pieces together, he won't make it. He may enjoy some early success, but as time marches on he will drift from the steady course of disciplemaking. Unless he understands *why* he is moving people through the stages of convert, disciple, laborer, and leader, plus *how* it is done, he will drift out to sea with all the others who minister without sharpened thoughts and methods.

A commitment of everything

After the twelve men returned from their first solo ministry assignment, Jesus concentrated on deepening the intensity of their conviction. Conviction, ministry skills, and supervisory attention form the three essentials that set apart the equipped laborer from the established disciple. Jesus accomplished this solidifying of his men through the feeding of the five thousand, the walking on water episode, and more conflicts with the religious establishment.

After miraculously feeding four thousand more people, the Master confronted his disciples with their absurd statement about having no bread (Mark 8:16). Imagine being in the boat with the Bread of Life and saying that we have no bread. However, regardless of their apparent dullness of spirit, the disciples were learning. Jesus continued to move the pieces of the puzzle around in their minds, and slowly they began to put those pieces together.

Deepening of conviction is vital because at some point dedicated laborers must deal with some of the more costly truths of the faith. Jesus was prepared to unload all the implications of commitment on his men. But it wasn't until ten months before the end of his earthly ministry that he spoke of giving up everything and going to the Cross.

Jesus' classic statements on the cost of discipleship were all made within the last ten months of his earthly ministry

(Mark 8:31-38, Luke 9:22-25, 9:57-62, 14:25-35). He broke the news to the disciples immediately after Peter's grand confessional that Jesus was the Messiah (Mark 8:29).

> He then began to teach them that the Son of Man must suffer many things and be rejected by the elders, chief priests and teachers of the law, and that he must be killed and after three days rise again. He spoke plainly about this. (Mark 8:31-32)

Jesus began to teach them something so different, so radical, so shocking that if he had told them any earlier, they probably would have turned away. Telling too much, too early can be devastating to a young believer's spiritual life. Many a good prospect for laboring has been ruined by well-meaning, assertive types who think new Christians should be as excited about sacrifice as they are.

What Jesus spoke to his men about suffering and dying was incomprehensible to them, and yet it was unchangeable. The disciples realized this fact when he set his mind to go to Jerusalem in order to obey and accomplish his Father's will. The remainder of Christ's ministry was simply a trip to Jerusalem.

The true cost of discipleship has created great interest throughout Church history. Various definitions and opinions of what it means to follow Jesus have been expounded. But there are certain nonnegotiable requirements involved in such a commitment.

The first requirement is *to think like Jesus.* Jesus thought with commitment. The Master said that he *must* suffer. There were no other options. It was as prophetically absolute as "It is written" or "Thus says the Lord." Jesus detailed what had to be done *by him alone:* He had to suffer, be rejected, be killed, and rise again (Mark 8:31). If only disciples could be as resolute about their lot as was the Discipler.

The mission of the Cross was bigger than Jesus himself in terms of his own personal, human desires to avoid the pain, the suffering, and the humiliation; but then God's purpose always is. The irresistible pull of his fate—that he must suffer, die, and rise again—was the eternal weight of divine mission that rested on Jesus.

The Master pulled no punches with his disciples; he was speaking plainly. And no one could misunderstand the meaning of his words, not even Peter. Peter's mind was spinning; he was fit to be tied. Probably he was thinking, "We just found out for certain that he is the Messiah, and now he drops *this* on us!" Peter was totally unprepared for this news; he was speechless—almost! He took the Lord aside and attempted to talk some sense into him. He rebuked his own Master!

One can only imagine what Peter said: "Lord, tell me it isn't true! What use is your kingdom if the King is dead? The Messianic kingdom means victory, the regal reign of the King! The Messiah can't fail! Tell me this isn't happening!" To Peter it was as if he had penned a wonderful novel and had set the type, but someone had come in overnight and rearranged it, and that saboteur was the King himself! This situation revealed the impetuosity of Peter. He was intoxicated with the heady wine of self-importance—the first among equals, the perceptive disciple who had just finished delivering his splendid confessional on the deity of Jesus.

The response of Jesus was quick and stinging: "Out of my sight, Satan!" (Mark 8:33). It was a bit strong, some might say, to use the name of Satan. But the gravity of the situation called for controlled rage on the part of Jesus in order to communicate the priority of his mission. Jesus said, "I must go!" but Peter protested, "No!" The Master knew that any effort to prevent the divine necessity of the Cross was a work of Satan. Why? Because Satan knew very well that the salvation of mankind was at stake. Ironically, Peter was the first disciple to declare that Jesus was the Messiah, and yet it was he who first committed this grievous sin of encouraging him to turn from the Cross.

It is frightening to see how easily we can suddenly take on the perspective of Satan. This happens when we try to keep others from doing God's will. One of Satan's most effective strategies is to get Christians to consider their own self-interest as equivalent to God's will. What better ploy than to push our selfish desires under the banner of the Cross.

Jesus accused Peter of having the wrong mind-set— setting his mind on man's interest rather than God's. When God says *must,* then we have to set our minds on doing his will, regardless of our feelings. This could mean turning down a promotion, or it could mean sacrificing certain pleasures for a meaningful devotional life. God has spoken plainly concerning what we *must* do. Even if it doesn't make any sense to us, we are called as his disciples to obey his plan.

Thinking like Jesus concerning the musts of ministry is essential to success. Temptations to drift away from the core of the mission confront us daily. Jesus could have engaged in many good works on this earth, conveniently forgetting the Cross. But then his work would have been in vain. Jesus taught the disciples that right thinking about ministry means staying true to what must be done, those things of divine necessity that are nonnegotiable. The Cross was a heavenly Nonnegotiable.

A second crucial dimension in the matter of following the Master is that *thinking like Jesus will lead to acting like Jesus.* An interesting event took place right after Jesus rebuked Peter. The Master invited the crowd to join him and his disciples as he expanded his thoughts on the cost of disciple-ship (Mark 8:34). This invitation effectively shows that disci-pleship is potentially for everyone. Jesus wanted more than just a small, elitist band of men to follow him. He started drawing the lines of discipleship by saying, "If *anyone* would come after me, he must deny himself and take up his cross and follow me," meaning that only those who will not make the commitment are excluded, and, really, they exclude themselves. The core of the Great Commission is to "make disciples" out of those who are willing to engage themselves in true commitment. Discipling is not exclusive or elitist. It is demanding, calling on people to change, to be disciplined, and to be held accountable to God and to others in their spiritual lives.

When Jesus mentioned self-denial and cross-bearing, what did he really mean? (Mark 8:34). Many think of self-denial as giving up something during the Lenten season. Others have said that it is to be dead to self, or even to hate self. I disagree with these opinions. When Jesus referred to self-denial, he was not talking about denying ourselves some luxury item or denying the reality of self or the needs of self. Rather, he was focusing on the importance of renouncing self as the center of our life and actions. In other words, self-denial is the decision of each of his followers to give over to God his body, career, money, and time. A true disciple is willing to shift the spiritual center of gravity in his life. *Self-denial is a sustained willingness to say no to oneself in order to say yes to God.*

Richard Wurmbrand, who spent fourteen years in Communist prisons, including three years in solitary confinement thirty feet below ground level, described his wretched condition of being cold, hungry, and in rags. "They broke four vertebrae in my back, and many other bones. They carved me in a dozen places. They burned and cut eighteen holes in my body. Yet, alone in my cell . . . I danced for joy every night. I discovered a beauty in Christ that I had not known before."[1]

The apostle Paul learned how to apply the peace of Christ to any situation. Self-denial was what he was talking about when he wrote, "I die daily." Whether it be Paul in prison, Christ in Gethsemane, or *you* under pressure on your own spiritual testing ground, self-denial is the willingness to say no to yourself in order that you might say yes to God.

The other side of the same coin is taking up one's cross. If a Jew saw a man with a cross on his shoulder, he could tell that the man was preparing to die. Once the cross had been picked up, there was no turning back. Some interpret the cross to be some personal hardship: a bossy in-law, a loud neighbor, or the daily traffic jam. We often hear the phrase spoken in jest: "Oh well, we all have our crosses to bear."

But a cross represents something more. It is the symbol of mission, the essence of purpose. Certainly it was Jesus' number-one assignment. It was what he said he *must* do. The Cross was the core of his life's work, something he could not avoid.

Whatever mission God gives me is my cross. If it is totally enjoyable, I enjoy. If it includes hardship, then I will endure it. Regardless of the assignment, taking up my cross means giving up many of my rights. I determine to see it through. I'm ready to die for it; I'm ready to live through it. There is no turning back—I'm totally committed.

Dietrich Bonhoeffer stated, "When Christ calls a man, He bids him to come and die."[2] The attitude of dying to self is exemplified in the story of the brave soldier who served under the Greek general Antigonus. This young soldier had a disease that was extremely painful and likely, at any time, to destroy his life. In every campaign he was in the forefront of the hottest battles. His pain prompted him to fight in order to forget; his expectation of death caused him to court death on the field.

Antigonus so admired the bravery of the man that he

had him cured of his malady by a renowned physician. From that moment the valiant soldier was no longer seen at the front. He avoided danger instead of seeking it, and sought to protect his life instead of risking it on the field. Just as his tribulation had made him fight well, his health and comfort destroyed his usefulness as a soldier.

The once-brave soldier had taken back possession of his life. Whenever the disciple takes back full control of his life, his effectiveness is sharply curtailed. Don't let anything get in the way of following Christ—not boyfriend, girlfriend, husband, wife, children, job, education, sports, hunting, fishing, bowling, hobbies, food, drink, house, vacations, or anything else.

What does it mean to follow Jesus? It means to *think* like Jesus and to *act* like Jesus. But there is one more aspect we must consider: *to invest like Jesus.* God gave us a life to spend, not to save. Investment refers to the wise expenditure of one's life. "For whoever wants to save his life will lose it, but whoever loses his life for me and for the gospel will save it" (Mark 8:35).

Many of us have this concept backward because we do not understand spiritual investment. Most often we try our best to save our life, and in doing so, we end up losing it. If this were not a problem, I doubt if Jesus would have brought up the subject.

The genesis of the self-help movement can be traced to Abraham Maslow's doctrine of self-actualization. Maslow's theory is built on what he calls a "hierarchy of needs." The most fundamental needs are physical ones, such as food and shelter. The second tier of needs are security needs, such as income and family. The third segment is love, and the fourth, purpose. According to Maslow's theory, only when these four layers of needs are met can a person be self-actualized, reaching his or her full potential.

Humanistically speaking, the self-actualization theory may appear to be true. Jesus, however, suggests that Maslow has it upside-down and backwards. For the Psychologist from Nazareth advocated that only in losing yourself can you find yourself. If you lose yourself in Jesus, then you will truly find yourself. It is a higher way; it is a harder way. He goes on to elaborate, "What good is it for a man to gain the whole world, yet forfeit his soul?" (8:36). The implication is, How much is your soul worth? What price are you willing to pay?

Jesus himself rejected the self-centered approach. He said no to self so that he could say yes to his Father and pick up his Cross. He invested his life in other men's souls—the most precious commodity on the face of the earth, for souls are eternal. Jesus is asking all those who follow him to make a similar investment. It will cost us something. Salvation itself costs us nothing, but discipleship will cost us everything.

Charlemagne attempted to put the Roman Empire back together again. He was a powerful man and a mighty general. His life's goal was to rule the world. When his grave was discovered, they found his skeleton seated on the throne with his bony finger pointing to a verse in the Bible that was on his lap. That verse read, "What would it profit a man if he were to gain the whole world and lose his own soul?" The obvious answer: nothing!

When one considers following Jesus, he must ask himself, What will the ledger sheet read at the end of my life? How much is my soul worth? Or my job, hobbies, relationships, moments of pleasure? Is there anything in my life that is preventing me from investing myself fully in the harvesting of souls? Jesus was telling this great multitude, "Don't throw your lives away! Follow me, think like me, act like me, and invest your lives like me. Lose yourselves in me and you will find everything you could ever need."

174 	COME AND BE WITH ME

Jesus should have a higher priority in our lives than family, possessions, and even self (Luke 14:25-35). Because the Master warned his twelve men of this radical cost of discipleship, they stayed with him in the face of difficulty, although others left (John 6:66-69). If a man is told that certain sacrifices are required of him, when adversity comes he will not be surprised or resentful. But if he is misled to think that all will be easy, then he will be both surprised and bitter. For this reason, a spiritual leader must be as honest and plainspoken as Jesus when explaining the requirements for successful ministry.

As Jesus pointed out, the bottom line of all ministry effort is the salvation of the soul (Mark 8:36). Even dedicated disciplers sometimes drift from center on this very issue. It is easy to get excited about those who are being established, the equipped laborers who arise, and the leaders who emerge from our work. But we must never forget that the primary goal of our ministry is the salvation of people. If discipleship does not include evangelism, it doesn't deserve the name discipleship.

This brings to a close our consideration of the "Come and be with me" phase of Jesus' ministry, a twenty-month intensive training period in which Jesus equipped many of his disciples to labor. Remember, an equipped laborer is an established disciple who has answered the call of God to labor by undergoing supervised training by an experienced leader. A laborer not only possesses ministry skills, but also has a deep commitment to help reach the world for Christ.

Footnotes:
1. Richard Wurmbrand, *Tortured for Christ* (Hodder and Stoughton, 1967), page 54.
2. Dietrich Bonhoeffer, *The Cost of Discipleship* (New York: Macmillan), page 7.

PART THREE
PRINCIPLES AND SUGGESTIONS

1. *The Church is called to make more disciples, to pray for more laborers, and to recognize leaders.* We have been commissioned by Jesus himself to make disciples (Matthew 28:19-20). A *disciple* is a believer who is established in the four fundamentals of God's word, prayer, fellowship, and witnessing. We are told to pray to God for more laborers in the harvest field (Matthew 9:38). A *laborer* is a disciple who has made a strong commitment to reach the world by ministering under the supervision of a leader in a church. A *leader* is a laborer who has proven his character through ministry experience and has been recognized by others as a person with leadership qualities.

2. *Establish a laboring team in order to achieve spiritual multipli-*

cation. Concentrate your time and attention on a few highly motivated and qualified disciples. Equip them with key ministry skills and responsibilities, gradually allowing them to minister on their own.

3. *Set three primary goals for your laborers: to possess deep conviction concerning the laboring task, to experience supervised training under the guidance of a mentor, and to learn and develop ministry skills.* Without a sense of resolution and commitment, disciples will not be able to withstand the pressures and challenges of independent work in the harvest field of ministry. Without a mentor to guide laborer-trainees, the important dimension of example, explanation, experiment, review, critique, and sharpening of skills will be absent in the training process. The need for skills is acknowledged by all builders of people. A seasoned laborer must understand Bible content and doctrine and must be able to carry out all the basic steps of evangelizing, establishing, and equipping.

4. *A laborer's character is a high priority in ministry.* A disciple must have integrity and emotional stability *inside* in order to successfully labor *outside* in the harvest field. If a disciple doesn't manifest substantial character, then be very careful about what kind of responsibility you entrust to him.

5. *Laborers need a philosophical grid.* The disciple-turned-laborer should be able to describe the underlying truths of discipling, along with the how-to's of translating theory into practice. At the end of the laboring process, he should be ready and able to outline and explain that whole process and the logic behind it.

6. *Establish a progressive training schedule with the simple, two-step method of observing and doing.* Give responsibility to laborers on a gradual, progressive basis. As they observe you modeling various facets of laboring, they will become confident enough to want to try doing it themselves.

7. *Effective equipping requires detailed instructions.* As you

provide specific details about the laboring process, you build confidence within your laborers. Basic guidelines do not quench freedom, but, on the contrary, they give growing laborers enough assurance and fortitude to exercise some self-expression and enthusiasm as they minister.

8. *Teach your laborers how to handle rejection.* Jesus did not react to rejection in a negative way, but turned the rejection into a lesson. Rejection is as much a part of ministry as praying or decision-making. Use it to your advantage.

9. *Focus on receptive hearts.* Don't waste time and spiritual truth on the unreceptive. Move with the movers; spend time with the spiritually motivated. Work on preventive medicine and train disciples to walk in the Spirit, bearing fruit for God.

10. *Show your laborers the true nature of proclaiming the word.* In his parable of the sower, Jesus described the responsibility of the laborer who spreads God's word to others (Mark 4:3-8, 14-20). His only responsibility is sowing; he is not responsible for the results, for that is God's business.

11. *Compassion is a key ingredient in spiritual multiplication.* Love, mercy, concern, and compassion all deal with the concept of personal attention. A laborer who truly cares about others will carry out his long-range ministry plans despite criticism from those who accuse him of neglecting immediate needs.

12. *Teach your laborers through personalized testing.* Jesus asked his disciples to do certain things that were essentially tests personalized to fit the need of the moment. You should be willing to do your testing through various means in order to refine the faith of each of your laborers. In this sense, ministry assignments are unique tools for the developing of unique people.

13. *The cost of discipleship is a truth that should be gradually unveiled to the disciple.* The commitment of Jesus' disciples grew slowly, but it did grow. The Master Disciplemaker did

not unveil too much too soon about the nature of the disciple-
laborer-leader progression. You will scare your disciples
away from ministry if you rush the pace of exposure.

14. *Successful laborers will interest others in becoming laborers.*
The success of Jesus' twelve disciples provided a positive
model for other disciples, creating a hunger within them for
more ministry. Make sure that your laborers are visible to
others within your church so that more interest is developed,
thus perpetuating the discipling-laboring process.

Part 4

YOU WILL REMAIN IN ME:
Leading

"If you remain in me and my words remain in you,
ask whatever you wish, and it will be given you.
This is to my Father's glory, that you bear much
fruit, showing yourselves to be my disciples."
John 15:7-8

11
THE CHARACTER OF A LEADER

Winston Churchill once said that there comes a special moment in everyone's life, a moment for which that person was born. That special opportunity, when he seizes it, will fulfill his mission, a mission for which he is uniquely qualified. In that moment he finds greatness. It is his finest hour.

When Jesus' hour had finally come, he was well prepared. But he was especially concerned for his twelve men, for he knew that they were not quite prepared to face the shock of the coming events. And yet the hour for which they were born would also be upon them very soon.

> It was just before the Passover Feast. Jesus knew that the time had come for him to leave this world and go to the Father. Having loved his own who were in the world, he now showed them the full extent of his love. (John 13:1)

The event Jesus had first mentioned to his disciples several months earlier had arrived. It no longer loomed as a distant trial or an abstraction of the mind. It was real, it was now.

What, then, was paramount on Jesus' mind with less than twenty-four hours before crucifixion time? Normally someone in his situation would probably ask, What is it like to die? How will I bear the pain of crucifixion? Is this really necessary? How can I get out of this?

But Jesus did not appear to be thinking any of these thoughts as he gathered his men around him. Rather, foremost in his mind was the condition of these twelve men. Scripture refers to them as "his own" (John 13:1), a term of endearment.

The Master was now ready to show his disciples "the full extent of his love." He loved them with all the love he had to give. They had been through a lot together. He had laughed with them, cried with them, ministered to needy people with them, and faced opposition with them. They had eaten together, prayed together, fought and fussed together. He had rebuked them, and they, in turn, had tried to rebuke him. But more than anything else, what characterized their relationship was love.

Why does God love us? We don't know; the Bible gives no final explanation. We just know that he does. It is an overwhelming mystery that God would take an interest in our experience.

But just as mysterious is the fact that Jesus wasn't thinking of himself at this moment of adversity. He was thinking of putting his finishing touches on the twelve's education. The basic field training under his leadership was now complete. Three years earlier, he had started his ministry by exposing some *curious converts* to the nature of ministry. This was the four-month "Come and see" period (Part 1). It was followed by the ten-month "Come and follow me" training period (Part 2), when these curious converts became *established disciples.* The third phase of training, "Come and be with me" (Part 3), was a twenty-month segment when those established disciples were transformed into *equipped laborers.*

But now, on this last day before his brutal crucifixion, Jesus gave the twelve a tightly packaged set of instructions, some essentials for leaders. He was now facing them with the hard facts, saying in essence, "You will no longer be with me. I am leaving. But first I want to tell you some essential principles that will make it possible for you to lead the thrust of the gospel into the world. These are the things you will need to grasp in order to make it in ministry." The Master wanted to show his men what kind of *character* a leader must have in order to effectively influence others. Jesus now began to cram three years into three hours. This represents the core of indispensable material for leaders. There was nothing extraneous about this evening.

A lesson in humility

The Master was not at all surprised to have arrived at the threshold of death. "Jesus knew that the Father had put all things under his power, and that he had come from God and was returning to God" (John 13:3). He knew where he had come from, where he was going, and why. He had no unmet needs; the Father had withheld nothing.

When a person's needs are met, he feels significant and secure; he doesn't try to dig his way out from underneath his own unmet needs. This significance and security form a basis for reaching out to others. Because Jesus himself had this kind of confidence, he was free to concentrate on his twelve disciples and on the work of his Father.

The Master had a real surprise for his men on this, the eve of his death. For he began his instructions on the essentials for leadership by donning a towel and washing the feet of his own disciples (John 13:4-12). Why would such an eminent man do such an eccentrically subservient thing? Washing feet was the exclusive task of the lowly servants. It seemed to be such a striking contradiction when Jesus slipped off his upper garment (giving him the appearance of a servant), wrapped himself in a towel, and did what *they* should have done. Actions do speak louder than words. Jesus had their full attention. What a powerful image: love on its knees washing feet.

When Christ came to Peter, an interesting scenario developed, for the brash disciple protested that he would not allow him to wash his feet (13:8). It was the ultimate incongruity for the Lord to wash the feet of his own servant. But Peter didn't seem to recognize that it was an even greater presumption for the servant to tell his Lord what to do. This wasn't humility that Peter displayed: it was pride. Peter knew that he wouldn't wash feet if he were God.

But the Master was showing his men the underside of leadership, the side that the world ignores: serving both the kind and the caustic, the meek and the mighty. This is the side of leadership that the disciples didn't want any part of, and didn't understand.

Jesus and Peter had totally different philosophies of leadership. The clash of wills there at that wash basin represents a significant contrast that exists even today between the humble leader and the leader who is too proud to "lower" himself enough to reckon with the dirt in other people's lives. Peter didn't want to accept this concept of leadership that serves, but Jesus insisted. The Master delivered a sharp rebuke when he said, "Unless I wash you, you have no part with me." In other words, If you don't allow me to do this, then get out! To reject this washing of the feet was to reject his approach to ministry. Jesus, by this powerful example, taught the twelve that if they wanted to lead, then they had to learn to humbly serve others.

Typically, Peter then moved to the other extreme: "Then, Lord, not just my feet but my hands and my head as well!" A moment earlier Peter had told Jesus he was doing too much; now he was doing too little! Jesus, however, was firm. The washing would go no further than the feet. They had already bathed, so a bath would have been redundant. Only their feet were soiled. There appears to be a double meaning here. The bath taken before dinner represents *justification*, the total cleansing from sin that takes place when in faith one accepts the righteousness of Jesus Christ. But the washing of the feet symbolizes the daily cleansing from our sin, or the process of *sanctification*. Daily, we are to confess our sins in order to be cleansed as we walk in the world. "If we confess our sins, he is faithful and just and will forgive us our sins and purify us from all unrighteousness" (1 John 1:9).

Jesus finished washing the disciples' feet, put on his garment, and returned to the table. Then he asked them a direct question: "Do you understand what I have done for you? You call me 'Teacher' and 'Lord,' and rightly so, for that is what I am" (John 13:12-13). Here Jesus reviewed his identity for them, a very crucial step. Why? Because if any other person had washed their feet, it would not have been quite so significant.

As an example of this, my wife will be cooking dinner this evening (I hope), but her efforts in the kitchen will not make the papers. However, some months ago we were told that President Reagan was to cook for several other world leaders. The simple act of cooking breakfast became front-page fare because of the cook's identity. What makes Jesus' act of washing feet important to leadership is the fact that he is Lord. Jesus prefaced his explanation with an identity review to give force to the lesson. The punch line of this lesson is found in verses 14 and 15: "Now that I, your Lord and Teacher, have washed your feet, you also should wash each other's feet. I have set you an example that you should do as I have done for you."

The words that stand out here are *should* and *example*. Are we willing to follow such an example? Many people would now stand in line to wash our Lord's feet. But what about the feet of others, those who have rocky marriages, rebellious children, shady business dealings, or hearts filled with hostility?

Instead of saying, "Wash my feet," Jesus said, "Wash one another's feet." My response to serving others is often, "I will if I must." In some perfunctory way I jam my brother's feet into ice water, or perhaps dry-clean his feet, hastily scraping off the dirt. To say my heart is in it would be stretching it. But the truth that melts away much of my resistance is that *Jesus washed Judas' feet,* even though he knew that the betrayal was near. If Jesus could wash Judas' feet, then I, too, can lead by serving others, even if many of them seem to deserve nothing more than judgment.

Washing feet also means forgiving others. And why should we forgive? Because the same spirit that repulsed Peter, causing him to hesitate to serve, is present within each of us. We all have within us those submerged continents of pride and lust that cry out for revenge, that desire to see people get what they deserve, that nurse grudges and feel like telling others off. But our calling is one of mercy, not of sacrifice and judgment.

Leaders must all beware the subtle plague of hypocrisy and self-righteousness. Our foremost impediment is pride— thinking that somehow we are better than our Master. But we should not focus on having power over others; rather, we should focus on *serving* others. Jesus didn't rearrange the pecking order: he abolished it! None of us would claim to be better than him. And yet we act as though we are. The ministry of the towel is a high calling because it is service in the tradition of our Lord.

Several hours later, Jesus donned not a towel but a cross in the greatest sacrifice of all. Indeed, his hour had come, and in his service he was glorified. The ultimate sacrifice was the ultimate service. In that servanthood, Jesus led the way for God's perfect will to be accomplished: the world's redemption. If Jesus had rebelled or exhibited selfishness, then God's redemptive plan would have been aborted.

How could we ever repay such a sacrificial act? Of course, we can't. But this we can do: When our hour comes, when it is time for us to answer his call, whatever he asks—*we can obey*. How could we possibly say no?

Jesus indelibly marked the minds of his disciples with this poignant example and explanation of leadership. There remained several other vital truths to be taught before he departed for Gethsemane, but none as memorable as this.

Love in action

We have all bled a little in our lives. We are indeed laden with character flaws that, if not shored up by the Spirit of God, could spell disaster and shame.

Probably Judas was a pretty good fellow. He had a good head on his shoulders. After all, the other men had elected him treasurer. But he was apparently rather superficial in his commitment to Christ.

When it became clear that Jesus would be tracked down and killed rather than being crowned King of Israel, Judas began to make secret plans for the future. The cracks in his character began to show. He had already been taking money from the treasury for his own purposes (John 12:4-6). He was laying aside a little nest egg for hard times, because trouble loomed large on the horizon. Like many insecure people,

Judas aligned himself with power. He had stayed close to the power of God for awhile, but now he was starting to deal with the enemy of God. After all, Jesus was going to die anyway. Why not turn a little profit?

Yes, Judas had seen the crippled walk, the lepers cleansed, the demon-possessed exorcised, and the blind receive their sight. He was in the boat when Jesus stilled the storm and walked on water. He, too, carried large baskets filled with leftovers after five thousand were fed by five loaves and two fish. Two days earlier he had witnessed Lazarus brought back from the dead. Just a few minutes earlier Jesus had washed his feet, as the Master choked back the tears.

Jesus was "troubled in spirit" that Judas, one of his twelve men, would betray him (13:21). He was troubled, agitated, disconcerted at the deepest level to know that one of his own was a devil. The Master's piercing eyes said it all. It never goes down easy that someone you have shown kindness and love to is going to turn on you and become your enemy. The prophetic statement Jesus called on to substantiate his charge is found in Psalm 41:9: "Even my close friend, whom I trusted, he who shared my bread, has lifted up his heel against me" (John 13:18-27). Jesus knew firsthand the sorrow, grief, and even the anger of betrayal.

The disciples were beside themselves. They were "at a loss to know which of them he meant" (13:22). Each of them wondered, "Is it I?" A healthy distrust of oneself is recommended so that we can recognize the dark potential of fallen human nature. A seasoned leader understands the ebb and flow of this fragile nature in others and in himself.

There was a heavy tension in the Upper Room. An oppressive feeling hung in the air. The anxious interchange between the twelve turned toward Jesus: Peter and John asked him directly the identity of the traitor. Jesus responded to their question by reversing the meaning of the customary practice of singling out an honored guest. When Jesus dipped his bread and handed it to Judas, it was not a gesture of honor, but of shame. Immediately Satan entered Judas to energize him for the final act. Jesus then commanded Judas to quickly go about his business.

It is interesting to observe the disciples' response. They thought Judas went out for groceries. They didn't even have a clue that this man left the room to inform against their beloved Master. Here we see the difficulty in discerning the true believer, even at the point of utter betrayal, even among well-taught laborers. How could they have been so naive? They had lived with Judas for nearly three years, yet they had never seen his traitorous character flaws.

Judas had played the role, knew the right words, the right prayers, the right actions. But it was only superficial; there was no taproot, no supernatural source in his life. One of the leader's daily realities is working with those who play the role. They will talk right, act right, and look right. But, as in the case of Judas, when the crunch comes, they will fold, and they will sell you up the river in order to save their own skin.

What must be understood in all this is the wonderful potential for good and the treacherous potential for evil resident in each of us. Here is a true story illustrating this point very well: Leonardo da Vinci had difficulty finding models for the faces of Jesus and Judas when he was painting his renowned "Last Supper." He finally found what he considered a right face for Christ. Years later, the only face he had not yet painted was that of Judas. One day while walking in the slums of his city, he found a man with a face filled with hate, lined deeply with the struggles of life. The artist had never seen a sadder man. The man sat for the painting, and when da Vinci finished, he asked the man his name. The man said, "Don't you remember me? Several years ago you used my face as the face of Christ."

One who a few years earlier seemed so righteous now appeared exceedingly evil. A wise man who leads doesn't forget that a little of Judas resides in all of us: that superficiality that makes it easy to jump on the bandwagon of apparent success or victory; that tendency to sell out to the highest bidder. It can't be emphasized enough that one of leadership's most important skills is the ability to recognize and discern those among us who allow the Judas in them to take control.

Jesus was troubled. But after the door had slammed and the faint sound of Judas' footsteps were no longer heard, Jesus said, "Now is the Son of Man glorified and God is glorified in him" (13:31). The time had come. *Now* the Son of Man would be glorified. The time was now because Jesus' hour of both shame and glory was upon him. The accomplishment of God's will was taking place right on schedule.

The traitor had been dismissed, and the atmosphere of the room changed dramatically. If you have ever been in a group where there was someone who didn't fit, you probably noticed that people were restrained, hesitating to say all they were thinking; but then, when that person left, everyone relaxed and the group turned to a more natural tenor.

Jesus reserved the main body of his Upper Room discourse for the faithful. The disciples were now purged of the traitor; now the secrets to success in ministry could openly be shared with those who had proven worthy to lead. Jesus reminded the eleven of his imminent departure: "My children, I will be with you only a little longer. You will look for me, and just as I told the Jews, so I tell you now: Where I am going, you cannot come" (13:33).

He had been telling them for ten months that he would die and leave them. It must have been difficult for him to say to his men, "I'm leaving you now; you're on your own. You're losing your Example and Leader. You need to cut the umbilical cord, to try your wings. Do not worry: I've prepared you for this. You can't go with me, but you *can* carry on my work right here." This was the encouragement of the Professor to his prize students on graduation day.

We can learn much from Jesus about the art of releasing people into leadership. Discharging disciples into ministry, particularly when their mentor is leaving, should never be a surprise. The Lord's disciples were not really surprised, and yet they still had difficulty accepting the transition. Although the Master had given them advance notice, as with the death of a loved one a person can only be so ready. When the reality hits, it does exactly that—it shakes us with new feelings and emotions that were impossible to prepare for.

The transition process to leadership must be gradual. Remember, these eleven men had been through approximately three years of training by the greatest Teacher who ever lived. He had established them as disciples and equipped them as laborers. Now he was teaching them the essentials of leadership. One sure way to scuttle God's plan for spiritual multiplication is to ignore the careful way Jesus prepared his men for his departure.

But what is the way to *succeed* in God's plan? Jesus answered this question with a new ministry directive.

> "A new command I give you: Love one another. As I have loved you, so you must love one another. All men will know that you are my disciples if you love one another." (John 13:34-35)

What is new about this command is not that people should love one another. This concept of loving one's fellow man was stressed long before this in the Old Testament (Leviticus 19:18). What is new in Jesus' directive is the striking phrase, "As I have loved you." Our example for loving people is Jesus himself! But the model of his love is one of principle, not of personality.

We don't know very much about the personality of Jesus. We have no audiovisual films to demonstrate his body language, facial expressions, and tone of voice, all of which comprise more than seventy percent of the communication process. But these factors don't matter so much anyhow when it comes to love. True love comes in all kinds of packages. If a person is reserved and not overly expressive, people often assume he is not loving, that he doesn't care. On the other hand, the "huggers" and expressive personalities are often considered to be loving and concerned. But these conclusions are made largely by focusing on personality rather than principle.

The principles that measure love are the same regardless of personality or style. Love is a verb, something that can be seen in action (1 John 3:16-17). It is the ministry of washing feet. It is something you do.

Jesus said, "If you love me, you will obey what I command" (John 14:15). Love has an objective measuring stick: If someone loves you, the evidence will be revealed in his actions toward you. The Master was telling his men, "I love you. I am even willing to go to the Cross for you. Now you must start treating each other the same way I've treated you. As a result, people will *know* that you are my disciples."

Don't consider others less loving just because of their personality. Determine love in spite of personality, based on the principles we find in Scripture. Jesus was saying that the world will not sit up and take notice of his followers if we have merely a personality love. Only a principled love is enough to establish credibility. And the only kind of people who are truly able to love as Jesus loved are disciples. Only disciples have the spiritual stomach for such a calling, having been established in God's word, prayer, fellowship, and witnessing.

Jesus wasn't talking about superficial love; there's plenty of that around in the world. Jesus was talking about loving even our enemies, the tough love assignments that a committed disciple alone can handle. Many of us readily agree that love is the most important part of Christian faith. But then the crunch comes, and that love breaks down; it fades in the stretch.

What is essential for disciples to grasp is that principled love alone makes the difference. Principled love is what caused Jesus to remain true to his mission, to willingly sacrifice himself for our sins, to earnestly train the twelve for ministry. Judas and love go together because Judas represented one of Jesus' greatest challenges in loving. To speak of love without dealing with those we despise is not to speak of love at all. If we truly love one another with the knowledge of both the ebb and the flow of human nature, of its potential for both good and evil, then only will the world's eyes be riveted to the Church.

The basis for confidence

The Master told his men not to be "troubled" (John 14:1). What did he mean by this? John Huss burned at the stake, but he was not troubled. Polycarp was thrown to the lions, yet he wasn't troubled. Jesus the Messiah was hung on a cross, but he was not defeated by his circumstances. One can be shaken or troubled over an athletic event, while at the same time another can be at peace in the face of death.

"Do not let your hearts be troubled," Jesus said. The reader might protest here, "That's easy for the apostles! They had Jesus!" But before we go too far, we must remember that these eleven men were up to their ears in trouble. The most immediate example is Peter: he was in shock. Jesus had told his remaining eleven men that where he was going they could not come. But Peter would not accept this; he wanted to know *why* he couldn't come (13:36-37). He was probably thinking, "Lord, I've walked on water with you, stood on the mountain of Transfiguration with you . . . I've been with you at all the important moments. Why not now? I will give my life for you. Is that what you want?"

It is interesting what we *think* we are willing to do, but what the hard facts of reality prove we are *unable* to do. And, ironically, in most cases God isn't even asking us to do it anyhow. Jesus knew Peter better than Peter knew himself. Peter's presumption is a marvelous illustration of the unknown self. His devotion was basically unquestioned—at least in his own mind. But his impatience, mixed with a strong dose of self-reliance, caused him to overestimate his readiness for the cup of Christ. We should all consider Peter's attitude as we look at our own.

Once during the first year I was in ministry, I was en route to another city. During the flight, I had opportunity to discuss my future with an older, more experienced member of the ministry team. I told him I was bored with giving three-minute testimonies, and was sure I was ready for the pastorate. This friend disagreed with me and told my why. "Bill," he said, "first, you don't know the Bible well enough; second, you're not mature enough; and third, you're not experienced enough." I was angry. Obviously this guy didn't know what he was talking about, I thought. But now, years later, I thank God that there was someone willing to tell me the precious truth, thus protecting me from myself.

Jesus stunned Peter, much like my wiser friend stunned me, with a startling confrontation: "Will you really lay down your life for me? I tell you the truth, before the rooster crows, you will disown me three times!" (13:38). Jesus was forcing his bold apprentice to confront the unstable nature of false confidence.

Peter was smashed. For one awful moment he saw himself in the mirror—his presumption, his pride, and his need to control the situation. Like an eyewitness to a shocking atrocity, he stood silent, somehow unable to speak.

If any group had reason to be troubled, it was the eleven. Men who had given up everything for their Master, and now they learn that they are losing him! In a short time they would collapse amid the chaos around them.

But in spite of all this, and in the face of it, Jesus told them, "Trust in God" (14:1). Most things, most people prove to be untrustworthy. But here was something solid on which they could base their trust: God himself. "This," the Master was telling them, "is where your confidence should lie."

But what about the future? they wondered. Jesus reassured his men that they should go about the business of his kingdom, and that everything they were concerned about would then take care of itself. Besides, there would be a place for them in heaven after they left the harvest field of this earth. Jesus told them, "In my Father's house are many rooms. . . . I am going there to prepare a place for you. And if I go and prepare a place for you, I will come back and take you to be with me that you also may be where I am" (14:2-3).

Jesus promised that there was a place for them. Not only was there plenty of room, but it was tailor-made for them.

For all those who know Jesus Christ as Savior and Lord, these words of Jesus, "Do not let your hearts be troubled. . . . I am going to prepare a place for you," are words of great comfort. But to a vast throng the uncertainty remains. If Christ were to ask, "Why should I permit you entrance into heaven?" their answer would be seasoned with good humanistic ideas, all of which will be to no avail.

The disciples needed assurance and Jesus saw to it that they got it. A second certainty he revealed to them was that *there will be a reunion.* They would someday see each other again in the heavenly realm (14:3). One of life's great hopes is that one day we will be reunited with loved ones. The pain and loneliness of separation is only temporary.

Not long ago I knelt beside my grandmother in the room where her husband of sixty-three years lay in a casket. I whispered into this frail, blind woman's ear, "You will see him again. You'll be together forever."

This is what the disciples needed to hear as they were feeling the agony of impending separation. Jesus, sensing this, assured them that he would come back for them and bring them all together for a big reunion. The Master anchored his men in the only secure harbor. He told them to place their confidence in *God* alone, for both the present and the future. He demonstrated that only in active humility and love can a laborer become an effective leader of others.

12
UNITED WITH GOD

If you had but a few hours left on earth to cement a limited number of truths in your disciples, what would those principles be? For Jesus those principles all focused on qualities that he himself exhibited, such as humility, love, and obedience. The Master encouraged his eleven leadership candidates to be spiritually in tune with him so that they would be in tune with God (John 14:6-14).

Jesus made many claims about his identity, but the crown of his claims is the series of great "I am's." The Gospel of John records eight such statements. The one that caused the greatest consternation among the religious establishment was his statement, "Before Abraham was born, I am!" (8:58), for here Jesus was claiming his own eternal pre-existence and equality with the Father. His most radical claim was, "I am the way and the truth and the life" (14:6). In the other "I am's," Jesus identified himself as "the bread of life" (6:35), "the light of the world" (8:12), "the gate" (10:7-9), "the good shepherd" (10:11), and "the resurrection and the life" (11:25). And in order to explain spiritual fruitfulness, Jesus said, "I am the true vine" (15:1-8).

The organic link

As they left the upper room and stepped out into the night air, the Master and his loyal eleven made their way to the Garden of Gethsemane, passing by some vineyards on the way (Mark 14:32, John 14:31). Jesus utilized the figure of the vine in an allegory about dependence on him.

Allegory is the description of a spiritual reality by means of the image of a physical reality. This was nothing new to the disciples, for Jesus often taught spiritual truth based on common images, such as bread, light, etc. The image of the vine can be found in abundance in the Old Testament, fifteen times in Ezekiel alone. Almost without exception, the vine represents Israel, and almost always casts a negative light on Israel, symbolizing its spiritual degeneration. Thus, when Jesus said, "I am the true vine," the disciples would automatically relate it to the spiritual life of Israel, or the lack of it.

In this allegory of the vine (John 15:1-8), Jesus is the vine, the Father is the gardener, and the disciples are the branches.

The vine and branches are parallel to Christ and his Church. Between the Master and his Church there is a mystical and spiritual union. The Church is organically joined to Christ just as the branch is joined to the vine. As the vine gives nourishment to the branch, so Christ, as the spiritual Head, provides nourishment to the body. This organic union is spoken of ten times in John 15:1-11 as "remaining." The Greek word *menō*, translated "remain" or "abide," means to dwell in or to make a home in. The eventual result of remaining is *fruit-bearing*.

Jesus explained the Father's (the gardener's) job description by saying, "He cuts off every branch in me that bears no fruit, while every branch that does bear fruit he trims clean so that it will be even more fruitful" (15:2).

The gardener does two things: he completely *removes* the dead, unfruitful branches and he *prunes* the good branches. Pruning is normally a semiannual process of cleaning the branches. Even the good branches need to be rid of "sucker shoots," or extraneous foliage. If these sucker shoots are not cut off, they take away much of the nourishment from the fruit.

There is often a steady growth of "sucker shoots" in our lives. When left unchecked, these spiritual appendages hinder and eventually stop growth of good fruit. Money and success can lead us to greed, and knowledge can become a source of pride. Therefore, God employs a kind of positive discipline—*pruning*—in order to increase our effectiveness in his service.

Because of this spiritual pruning process now, we will bear more fruit in the future. A leader must be willing and sensitively able to assist God in this operation, challenging disciples (the branches) to be more fruitful. But in order to be fruitful, each branch must be united with the vine, Jesus himself, who said, "Remain in me, and I will remain in you. No branch can bear fruit by itself; it must remain in the vine. Neither can you bear fruit unless you remain in me. . . . If anyone does not remain in me, he is like a branch that is thrown away and withers" (15:4,6).

A vine is good for nothing unless it bears fruit. A life not bearing fruit is a useless life; it does not *remain* in Jesus. There are several things one can do without remaining in him: hold a job, raise a family, serve on a church board, even pastor a church. But *without being united with Christ we cannot bear fruit*. And if we do not bear fruit, then all our efforts are futile and our lives in vain.

Jesus went on to say, "If you remain in me and my words remain in you, ask whatever you wish, and it will be given you" (15:7). His "words" were given to the disciples as food for spiritual growth. The written revelation of Scripture—God's *word*—is important primarily because the principles taught therein lead to spiritual freedom. For as Jesus stated earlier in his ministry, "If you hold to my teaching, you are really my disciples. Then you will know the truth, and the truth will set you free" (8:31-32).

Getting environmentally high won't free us, a sensual experience won't do it, procedures and policies won't do it, determination won't do it—only truth revealed from God's word will set us free. Many evangelicals scramble wildly to find an easy way out of basic growth requirements. The fact that five hundred well-meaning Christians will fill a sanctuary to hear a singing group but stay away constantly from Bible study is a testimony to our fallen nature. It is simply easier to dance in the Spirit than to study, easier to hold hands and sing along than to wrestle with God in prayer.

The choice of Christians to remain in Christ is primarily a choice about God's word. The right decision is the one made by Ezra. "For Ezra had devoted himself to the study and observance of the Law of the Lord, and to teaching its decrees and laws in Israel" (Ezra 7:10).

To have God's word abiding in us begins with the choice to study the word, to practice the word, and finally to teach the word. It should be our goal to be established in the word, having a working knowledge of the content of Scripture and the ability to apply it to life (2 Timothy 2:15). The primary solution to our estrangement from God is study, study, study of his word.

Too many professing Christians have a superficial understanding of the faith, characterized by understanding Christianity in bits and pieces, thinking of it as better personal behavior with a good retirement plan. As long as Christians think of Christianity as merely a better way of life or a better version of man's relationship to God than most other religions, we will get nowhere! People's minds need to be radically changed through a regular, supernatural encounter with the word of God. This forms the foundation of the Christian life.

The believer who *remains* in Christ will not only interact with Scripture, but he will also *pray*. Jesus tells us, "Ask whatever you wish, and it will be given you" (15:7). This is quite a promise. An informed, word-filled believer will pray intelligently and will, more often than not, be within the will of God. What is being taught here is a commitment to communicate with God. Talk to God in prayer and he will talk back to you in his word. The only way one person gets to know another is by communicating. We are called to communicate with our God on a regular basis. This, too, is part of the process of being united with the vine.

The battle for spending meaningful time with God is fought on three fronts: priorities, scheduling, and discipline. A recent survey of Christian leaders revealed a number of reasons for difficulty in maintaining a regular devotional life with God: thirty-four percent said *time* was the greatest problem, nine percent said *distractions,* seven percent said *consistency,* and six percent cited the difficulty of *discipline.*[1]

In order to remedy this problem, we need to make our personal time with God an objective to keep, prioritizing it by placing it in our schedule and then disciplining ourselves to live by that schedule, knowing that the end result will be satisfying. Communicating with God leads to knowing God, and knowing God leads to obeying God.

Another important way to be united with God is in our *obedience.* Jesus went on to say to his loyal followers, "As the Father has loved me, so have I loved you. Now remain in my love. If you obey my commands, you will remain in my love, just as I have obeyed my Father's commands and remain in his love" (15:9-10). If we respond to the Father's love with obedience, not only do we prove our love, but we also *remain* in God's love. The obedience theme is repeated five times in chapters fourteen and fifteen (14:15,21,23, 15:10,14). God desires obedience before anything else; it is first on his agenda.

But obedience is not a simple, clear-cut legalism. Augustine said, "Love God and do whatever you please." Some don't like that statement because of the "do whatever you please." That type of freedom makes us squirm, giving rise to a sense of insecurity. A system of do's and don'ts is, in a sense, safer. But to resist freedom in Christ is to both misunderstand and underestimate loving God. Loving God *is* obeying God. The power of love is awesome. It has given birth to more courageous acts than fear, doubt, and laws ever will. The only enduring motive for obeying God is love. Any other motive will degenerate into perfunctorily going through the motions.

But knowing, loving, and obeying God is a full-time pursuit. E.M. Bounds wrote, "The men who have most fully illustrated Christ in their character, and have most powerfully affected the world for Him, have been men who spent so much time with God as to make it a notable feature of their lives."[2] God's character should be our character.

The fruit of the Spirit should be produced by the Christian as he naturally grows into the image of Jesus Christ. Some students of Scripture pit the character fruit of Galatians 5:22-23 against ministry fruit, or the results of laboring: converts, disciples, and other tangible advancements. Drawing this distinction is like trying to separate being and doing, which is spiritually impossible. Ministry fruit is a natural byproduct of the fruit of the Spirit.

When we bear spiritual fruit, we glorify God (15:8). We give him *joy*, which in turn gives us joy (15:11). The reward for obedience is joy, which I define as a sense of well-being as a result of a job well-done. Joy is the inner knowledge that, regardless of circumstances, I am pleasing God. Joy is not happiness; happiness is at the mercy of happenstance. Joy, on the other hand, is present in any environment *if* obedience is present.

Jesus finds joy in seeing his disciples obey. When we succeed, it thrills God's heart. Not too long ago, my son hit a grand-slam home run in a Little League game. As he rounded the bases he jumped for joy, but his joy was small compared to the joy I felt for him. God is delighted when we obey him, and his joy supernaturally becomes our joy.

Later in his discourse, Jesus explained the eternal nature of joy. "Now is your time of grief, but I will see you again and you will rejoice, and no one will take away your joy" (16:22). The Christian's joy is eternal, untouchable, and rooted in the Resurrection of Jesus. No one can lock the Christian out of joy except the Christian himself. Joy is possible, regardless of difficulty, when *obedience* is present.

This is the essence of what God expects from us. He doesn't directly ask for our money, time, holidays, or favorite hobbies. He wants *us*. We are his children, and so he naturally wants our love and our obedience. Parents do not want their children's toys. Parents desire the love and loyalty of their children. When a child knows that he is loved, he won't hesitate to share his toys with his parents. When I know that God loves me, that he desires only the best for me, then I give him anything I own—because of love.

The issue, to God, is our choice of allegiance. If my

choice is to *remain* in him, as a branch in the vine, then I must commit myself to the word, prayer, and the obedient life. Then I will bear fruit, I will glorify God and have joy, and my life will count for something. What else could I ever ask for or expect? Could I ever ask for anything more than to be called his disciple?

Jesus revealed to his disciples the most dynamic information yet in the graphic allegory of the vine and branches. The fruitful Christian life, the ability to lead, and the possession of joy are rooted in him. He is the organic link to God, and to our fulfillment. The eleven now understood that effective leadership is based on an effective relationship with Christ, and that the relationship they were losing by his departure would in a sense deepen because it would no longer be limited by time and space. The disciples were beginning to see that instead of only possessing one pair of eyes, hands, and feet, now Jesus would multiply himself a myriad of times through converts who become disciples, then laborers, then leaders.

The Spirit of truth

A picture in a magazine shows a plain bar of iron worth $5.00. If the same iron bar were made into horseshoes, it would be worth $10.50. Fashioned into needles it would be worth $5,000, and into balance springs for watches it would actually be worth $250,000.

The secret is in how it is used. So, too, human beings. The Master Fashioner of lives can transform an individual into a valuable instrument of usefulness. See what giants of usefulness Jesus made of eleven disciples.[3]

For thirty-four months Jesus had perfectly orchestrated the training of his twelve men. The training had reached a critical stage as they neared the time for their release into leadership. The disciples were struggling with the uncertainty of the future and the anticipated absence of their leader.

The mood was solemn, as the Master noted: "Because I have said these things, you are filled with grief" (John 16:6). In a morbid state of gloom, the disciples were not very useful to anyone. They were completely preoccupied with the imminent separation. But now Jesus began to introduce vital ideas that would once again give his men a positive perspective on the future: "But I tell you the truth: It is for your good that I am going away. Unless I go away, the Counselor will not come to you; but if I go, I will send him to you" (16:7).

For the second time Jesus stated confidently that his departure would spell greater success for his followers. Unless Jesus departed, the Holy Spirit wouldn't come. If the Spirit didn't come, the disciples wouldn't significantly change, the work wouldn't multiply, and thus much of their training would have been in vain. Through the Master's followers the Holy Spirit would usher in a new era of spiritual blessing.

As so often happens, Christians' greatest gains come in our greatest losses. Disappointments, sickness, financial setbacks, and even divorces can bring new vistas of opportunity. The difficult part is seeing the good during the loss; it's much like trying to drive through thick fog. God delivers many wonderful packages during a Christian's lifetime, but some of those deliveries come through the back door of our lives.

Jesus' challenge was to convince the eleven that the advent of the Spirit would enhance his own influence greatly in the world. It would cause the disciples' lives to be more effective and joyful, for the Spirit's counsel and works would equal those of their Master. But as long as Jesus was around, his followers would probably pay little attention to the Spirit.

With Jesus around, human nature would not allow the Holy Spirit to have a full ministry. Jesus explained that he had to leave so that the Counselor could come and then the work of God's kingdom could expand. History teaches that people love progress but hate change. The disciples were no different; they resisted the passing of the baton and the new method of ministry. They frankly preferred Jesus to the Holy Spirit, Someone they had never met and did not understand.

Jesus insisted that the Spirit needed to come—but what would this Counselor do when he arrived? There are several ministries performed by the Spirit, most relating to the believer. There is, however, one prescribed work the Spirit fulfills in relation to the whole world. Jesus mentioned this function first: "When he comes, he will convict the world of guilt in regard to sin and righteousness and judgment: in regard to sin, because men do not believe in me; in regard to righteousness, because I am going to the Father, where you can see me no longer; and in regard to judgment, because the prince of this world now stands condemned" (16:8-11).

It was imperative for the disciples to understand that the hearts of men are continually being prepared for the gospel message. The three-pronged work of the Spirit brings the world to a knowledge of its sin, of the righteousness of Christ, and of the reality of a future judgment. The concept of God that the world needs is the concept that the Spirit teaches. The world must find its way from relative ignorance concerning the truth about God to a sufficient knowledge for an intelligent decision.

The world, having been duped by the devil, is spiritually dead and doesn't even know it. The Spirit's work is to bring people of the world to an overwhelming knowledge of sin, like a guilty defendant who is convicted inside when faced with incontrovertible evidence against him. Second, the Spirit makes the world aware of the righteousness of God through Jesus Christ and his Church. Third, the Spirit confronts the world with the certainty and the finality of judgment.

Jesus was giving his men confidence that when they went out to minister, some important groundwork by the Holy Spirit would precede them. But although the Spirit's ministry to the world is important information for the disciple, the ministry of the Spirit to the believer probably seemed far more vital to the eleven at this point.

In his discourse Jesus made a very interesting comment: "I have much more to say to you, more than you can now bear" (16:12). He couldn't tell them much more because they just couldn't bear it. Asking the disciples to carry the knowledge Jesus possessed about the future would be like asking a five-year-old to carry a refrigerator on his back. Jesus did withhold information from the twelve; he operated on a need-to-know basis.

A vital principle of leadership-development is, Do not back up your truck of truth and dump the whole load on the unprepared. Instead, learn the appropriateness of holding back your knowledge. Jesus was telling his disciples that he had barely scratched the surface with them. There was much more for them to know, but they were not yet ripe for the knowing.

This is where the Spirit comes in, for someday and in some way the disciples would need to be taught that "withheld truth" that Jesus was referring to. The Master began to tell the eleven of their new Teacher: "When he, the Spirit of truth, comes, he will guide you into all truth. He will not speak on his own; he will speak only what he hears, and he will tell you what is yet to come" (16:13).

Often people will say, "If only I could have been there with Jesus. If only I could have talked with him and known him as the twelve disciples knew him. Then my spiritual life would be better and my faith stronger." This idea is, quite frankly, a delusion. The disciples themselves proved that living with Jesus was no guarantee of a vital walk with Christ. Consider for a moment what made the crucial difference in the disciples' lives.

While Jesus was physically present on earth, he taught the disciples over and over. He orchestrated their training perfectly, yet they were perplexed with his teaching. He left them scratching their heads in confusion more often than not.

It was not just being present with Jesus that changed the disciples from a frightened bunch of spiritual interns to a mighty band of courageous leaders. What transformed these men was Pentecost—the outpouring of the Holy Spirit. And part of what the Spirit pours out is truth. He is like a tour guide who points out important portions of the spiritual terrain. He is indeed "the Spirit of truth."

Jesus continued with a description of the Spirit's teaching method: "He will bring glory to me by taking from what is mine and making it known to you" (16:14). The truth revealed by the Spirit is not just third-party information: it came from Jesus himself. The Spirit even reminds the believer of Jesus' words (14:26). He makes the necessary connection between the mind of God and the mind of man. He is a Counselor who can reveal to us even some of "the deep things of God" (1 Corinthians 2:10-16). He reveals truth itself. Abundant truth from the mind of God is found in the word of God, which was written by the Spirit (1 Peter 1:10-12, 2 Peter 1:21). When I read the word of God, the Spirit takes the truth and communicates it to me in a way I can apply to my life. The moment I begin to take action on the principles, the supernatural teaching ministry of the Spirit is taking place in my life. The Christian life, if healthy, is simply a series of these progressions.

Jesus promised his disciples that the Spirit would remind them of the important truths they were sure to forget. One of man's most common shortcomings is forgetfulness. The Scriptures are filled with exhortations to *remember* the Lord and all he has done for us. But how can we remember without divine help?

Most seasoned Christians are not in need of large segments of new truth, but rather need to be reminded of existing truth that can bring new meaning to their lives. It had to be comforting for the eleven disciples to recognize that many of the important lessons Jesus had taught them would come back to them in their moment of need. This is what the Spirit will do—guide the Christian into all the truth he needs to know, and remind him of all he needs to remember.

The Holy Spirit does not speak on his own initiative. He is not asked to be an autonomous or serendipity operator. What he hears, he speaks, for he is serving in the interests of Jesus (16:13-14). The Spirit's job is to bring glory to the Messiah. There is no self-aggrandizement in his work. The Spirit points not to himself, but to the One on the Cross. This spirit of the Spirit should be the spirit of the Christian: to glorify Christ.

The next comment of Jesus seems to pull together all the remaining pieces of the wonderful puzzle: "All that belongs to the Father is mine. That is why I said the Spirit will take from what is mine and make it known to you" (16:15).

What belongs to the Father and Son is actually given to me. It is like being told that the Colorado River is mine. The question is, How can I harness and utilize the potential power in the river? The answer is Hoover Dam, which daily produces many megawatts of electricity. But the power of the mighty Colorado channeled through Hoover Dam is only useful when it is released to me in a measured way, as when I flip a light switch or turn on my television. The Holy Spirit doles out the information and power that are the Father's, but he does so in meaningful increments that meet my needs.

Having access to the full-orb ministry of the Holy Spirit is like having everything you will ever need at your fingertips. The Christian can have the treasure, wisdom, and power of the Godhead at his fingertips.[4] The first step is to plug into the Source. Scripture tells us to be filled with the Spirit (Ephesians 5:18).

The eleven disciples were about to embark out into roles of *leadership* in the early Church. They needed to know the nature of their new Teacher for this coming phase of ministry. So Jesus explained who the Spirit was, why he was coming, what he would do for them, and how they could tap into the vast resource of his power. The relationship they had experienced with their Master had been wonderful. But now a new relationship was to be developed. In their great anticipation, they could only guess what it would really be like to have a relationship with this new Counselor in this new Church age, but their Master and Friend set their minds at ease.

Jesus thus gave a brief, one-day seminar on leadership principles. And what were his astute conclusions? What does it really take to lead? *Humility* of spirit, enabling a person to lead as a servant. *Love*, demonstrating to all the world that disciples are authentically commissioned by God. *Confidence* that there is a place for us in the future and that our Master will come back for us. *Prayer*, opening the door for limitless possibilities and a conversation with God at any time. *Obedience*, the proof of our love for God and the key to joy and fulfillment in the Christian life. *Fruitfulness,* a spiritual productivity that naturally results when we remain in Christ. Finally, *the Holy Spirit,* who guides, comforts, empowers, and teaches disciples of Jesus how to carry out the work of the kingdom of God.

The Master had given his little band of men over three years of discipleship training. But on this fateful evening, there in the Garden of Gethsemane, he finally released his disciples out into the world to labor and lead in his kingdom. Before the traitor arrived with the Roman executioners, the Master went off to make an impassioned plea to his Father while his weary men slept. But first he concluded his discourse with a beautiful benediction for all disciples:

> "I have told you these things, so that in me you may have peace. In this world you will have trouble. But take heart! I have overcome the world." (John 16:33)

There were events yet to take place during the course of the next few days that would cause these men to question the reality of the King as well as their ability to lead in his kingdom. They would be temporarily overwhelmed by the very world that their Master had so masterfully conquered. But the Spirit, their newly appointed Teacher, was soon to come to remind them of Jesus' words of encouragement. The new Counselor would bring many of the Master's words back to them as chords of hope ringing in their souls.

The three years spent with Jesus would expand as these eleven men would become hundreds, thousands, and millions. And so the mature fruit of discipleship has been progressively pruned and harvested throughout the ages—all to the glory of the One who started the whole process with a handful of average people like you and me.

Footnotes:

1. Terry Muck, "Ten Questions about the Devotional Life," *Leadership*, Volume 3, Number 1 (Winter 1982), page 31.
2. Bounds, *Power*, page 48.
3. Pulpit Resource, Volume 2, Number 3 (Byron, California: Glendon E. Harris, September 11, 1983), page 36.
4. The idea for this illustration came from Ray Stedman, *Secrets of the Spirit* (Old Tappan, N.J.: Fleming H. Revell).

PRINCIPLES AND SUGGESTIONS

1. *Before sending laborers out on their own, make sure they know what they will be facing.* The Upper Room discourse served as an encapsulated core of truth relating to Jesus' disciples and the nature of the leadership task before them. Such a seminar should be given to laborers in a retreat type atmosphere just before they embark on their solo mission of leadership.

2. *True leadership consists of character, knowledge, and skills.* The basic elements taught by Jesus in his Upper Room discourse—humility, love, confidence, effective prayer, obedience, understanding of the Holy Spirit, and fruitfulness—are a combination of character traits resulting from applied knowledge. When put into practice, they are ministry skills.

214 YOU WILL REMAIN IN ME

Leadership is not just *doing* something; it is a combination of being and doing. Leadership is an ongoing, lifetime learning process.

3. *Humility is a vital key to effective leadership.* When Jesus got down on his knees to wash their feet, it made a lasting impression on his disciples. Someone who leads must also serve. Try to think of creative ways to serve the people you are training.

4. *Obedience is the proof of love.* Loving God is obeying God. Words alone do not demonstrate sincerity, dedication, and love. Consistent action is the best evidence of your concern as a leader.

5. *The love of Christians for one another is the most powerful form of evangelism.* Teach men to love each other in the same way that Jesus loved people. Such communal caring will demonstrate to unbelievers that these people truly follow God (John 13:34-35).

6. *Remaining in Christ entails regular Bible study, prayer, and obedience to God.* A leader cannot effectively serve God unless he is in constant touch with God. A regular daily intake of God's word enables him to speak to us, guiding us in all our ministry activities. Prayer is another form of constant communication with God. When our prayer dialogue stops, real spiritual growth stops. Our obedience enables us to put into effect God's plan for our lives.

7. *Make sure that you understand and apply the ministry of the Holy Spirit.* The Spirit guides leaders in the Church to truth and provides holy encouragement in times of trials and distress. Today's leader must be filled with and controlled by this great Counselor in order to serve in the crucible of ministry in this challenging age.

GLOSSARY OF TERMS

Convert: A believer in Jesus Christ; a regenerated person; an eternal member, by faith, of the family of God.

Disciple: A convert who is established or grounded in the four fundamentals of the Christian life: God's word, prayer, fellowship, and witnessing.

Laborer: A disciple who has accepted the call of God on his or her life to enter the harvest field; one who is making disciples via evangelism and follow-up training.

Leader: A laborer who has the gifts and training for leadership; a person who equips other laborers.

Minister: One serving in any form of ministry, whether a fresh convert, an active disciple, a skillful laborer, or an experienced leader; this term describes a function rather than a stage of development.

Discipler or disciplemaker: Someone who is making disciples or laborers, or who is training leaders.